Memoirs of a Celibate Priest

Memoirs of a Celibate Priest

Recollections of an Anglican Ministry

by

the Reverend Kenneth Eric Jarvis
Vicar of Beaulieu 1960 to 1977

JANUS PUBLISHING COMPANY
London, England

First published in Great Britain 1993
by Janus Publishing Company

Copyright © Kenneth Eric Jarvis 1993

**British Library Cataloguing-in-Publication Data.
A catalogue record for this book is available
from the British Library.**

ISBN 1 85756 098 1

Printed & bound in England by
Antony Rowe Ltd, Chippenham, Wiltshire.

Contents

Acknowledgements

I would like to record my thanks for help received from the
following individuals, organisations and books:

the Bishop of Chichester

the late Mrs Kathleen Coade

the late Captain H E Widnell, and his book *The Beaulieu Record*

the late Canon Colin Cuttell

the late Father Denis Marsh SSF, and his book *Father Algy*

Sussex by Arthur Mee

The Centenary History of St Mary's, Portsea: *Consecrated to
Prayer*

Portsmouth Evening News

The Oxford Dictionary of the Christian Church

The Community of the Resurrection, Mirfield, West Yorkshire

J M Dent & Sons for permission to quote from *Autobiography* by
Conrad Noel ed Sidney Dark

Toc H for permission to quote from *A Living Witness* by Kenneth
Prideaux-Brune

The extract from Hilaire Belloc's *The South Country* is reprinted
by permission of the Peters Fraser & Dunlop Group Ltd.

*Illustration for the jacket cover was taken from an old print of Beaulieu
Abbey Church.*

Foreword

These reminiscences are written in the reverse order, starting from where I am now, and going back to my earliest beginnings. This is how I remember things.

1
Sussex
1977–1992

I never get between the pines
But I smell the Sussex air;
Nor I never come on a belt of sand
But my home is there.
And along the sky the line of the Downs
So noble and so bare.

Hilaire Belloc

I am writing these lines on my eighty-sixth birthday. From the window of my bedsitting-room I look out to the rolling sweep of the South Downs, three miles away to the south. The smooth line of the whale-back ridge is not completely unbroken. It is marred by the ugly buildings of the Devil's Dyke Hotel. A mile to the west a line of unsightly electricity pylons loop their way over the crest of the downs; more serious than this, a television company was allowed to build a monstrous television mast, which would clearly have been prohibited if the planning authorities had been awake to their responsibilities.

At the foot of the downs, on the north side, there is a wonderful string of 'forgotten' little downland churches. Today they are either isolated or surrounded by a cluster of houses or a small hamlet. But for many centuries, when hundreds of thousands of sheep cropped the soft turf of the South Downs, there was a large population of shepherds and agricultural workers. Most of these churches were built soon after the Norman Conquest, but some go back to Saxon times.

Immediately under Ditchling Beacon, the second highest point of the South Downs, is Westmeston, a thirteenth-century church. Nearby is Ditchling, also a thirteenth-century church, standing opposite the gabled old house of Anne of Cleeves. From Ditchling can be seen the striking V of fir trees planted on the downs to celebrate the Jubilee of the Victorian era. A mile to the West is Clayton church, first built by the Saxons. Some of the earliest wall paintings in England, dating from the thirteenth century, can be seen on three walls of the nave and on the Saxon arch. Directly above the church are the Jack and Jill windmills, a very well known Sussex landmark, fortunately restored recently.

A mile to the west is the hamlet of Pycombe, dangerously near to the London-Brighton road. When I first came to live here, the old forge opposite Pycombe church was still at work. For many generations Pycombe forge made iron crooks for the shepherds of the downs. In more recent years, after the downs were largely ploughed up, Pycombe forge went on making shepherds' crooks, having built up a worldwide reputation for making crooks for twentieth-century bishops. Pycombe's other claim to fame is the leaden font, one of the largest leaden fonts in the country, supposed to have been made in 1170.

Continuing westwards, a mile away, is the little church of Newtimber, seven hundred years old and beautifully restored. Newtimber Place was the home of the Buxton family and, over the sixteenth-century pulpit in the church, there is a striking memorial to Lord Buxton's son, who was killed at the age of twenty, while leading his company into action in Flanders during the First World War. The words on the memorial are these:

> Young, gifted, radiant, most beloved, his very presence stimulated happiness and gaiety. Life promised him all that he held most dear, yet eagerly and steadfastly he gave himself for his country.

At Poynings church, two miles to the west, are memories of one of England's earlier wars. Michael Poynings built this church on coming home from Crécy. It is a splendid church with a massive tower, supported by four fine arches.

Continuing westwards, along the narrow little road that lies right under the steep escarpment of the downs, is Edburton church. The ancient lead font has been there for eight hundred years and the fathers of the men who made it may have seen William the Conqueror. Archbishop Laud gave the church its Jacobean pulpit and charming altar rails, and may well have preached from the pulpit himself.

Beyond the gap in the downs carved out by the river Adur is Buncton church, a little gem isolated in the surrounding fields. The hill on which it stands was given for a temple by Adewulf, King of the South Saxons, in 791. The tiny little Norman church is today much as it was when it was built. It has a noble chancel arch, through which can be seen the east window lancets. The light streams through these windows, as it did when King John signed Magna Carta.

Quite near is Wiston church, now rather neglected, in the grounds of Wiston House, for long the home of the Goring family. Above Wiston, on the crest of the downs, is Chancton-bury Ring, a famous landmark seen from all over the Sussex Weald. The real ring is an ancient circular earthwork with its rampart still visible, but most folk think of the great clump of beech trees which makes the site such a landmark. It is said that these were planted as saplings in 1762, by Charles Goring of Wiston House, who climbed the hill day by day to keep them watered. What a wonderful memorial! Alas, in the great gale of October 1987 many of these giants were blown down. New trees have been planted, but it will be many years before the great clump resumes the familiar shape that has been known to many generations.

Westwards, on the other side of the London-Worthing road, are Sullington, Storrington and Parham churches. Parham is one of the most magnificent houses in Sussex, set in a park of five hundred acres, full of cedars and great beech trees, with bracken and lily ponds, and with deer browsing right up to the house. The house is Tudor, built on an E-shaped plan, with walls faced by stone. The hall has four windows eight yards high and the whole house is light and airy. It is full of treasures, with splendid pictures and furniture and a gallery at the top of the house is a hundred yards long. The little fifteenth-century church is a hundred yards from the house. The old two-decker pulpit is still here and a room, or big box pew, to the north of the chancel, where the lord of the manor sat with his family, all warming themselves beside an open fire.

On the other side of the downs, south of Steyning, stand three ancient churches of exceptional interest. Botolphs church is a thousand years old, standing on the banks of the Adur near the Roman bridge which once spanned the river. Coombes church, a mile away, is hidden in a farmyard, but has been there for eight hundred and fifty years, with its two Norman doorways and Norman font. Sompting church, two miles to the south-east, has a Saxon tower, the only one of its kind in England, with a church built round it about nine hundred years ago. The tower, rising to a height of a hundred feet, has Roman bricks built into it.

Sussex is, indeed, most fortunate to possess such a wealth of interesting and beautiful churches, all in such a small area of the South Downs. Since my retirement, fifteen years ago, I have taken services from time to time in most of them. The Church of England today, with its shortage of priests and with many incumbents having charge of three or more churches, is very dependent on the services of the retired clergy. But I have found it a great privilege to be allowed to conduct services in such wonderful old buildings, where 'prayer has been valid' for centuries.

One of my happiest memories is of driving along a dark, twisting and narrow country road on Christmas Eve, and then arriving at Edburton church for the Midnight Mass, where the church was ablaze with soft candlelight and full of welcoming country folk.

After I had been retired for about five years and was feeling I was not sufficiently extended, I wrote to the chaplain of Lewes Prison and asked if I could be of any use to him. He replied, saying that he was looking for a part-time deputy chaplain, who could stand in for him on his days off and be responsible for his duties when he was away on holiday, sometimes for several weeks at a time.

After a few weeks on probation, and after careful security checking, I was duly appointed deputy chaplain.

I would drive the twenty miles to the prison and, on arrival, would be given, by the warder in charge of the main door, a master key which had to be attached by a chain to my belt and, of course, surrendered when I left the prison. One of the things I found hard to remember at first was that, after going through a door (and the prison has many doors), the door had not only to be closed, but locked. The key also gave entrance to all the prisoners' cells.

It is the duty of the chaplain to visit, each day, the prisoners in the prison sick-bay, or hospital. New arrivals must be visited as soon as possible after they arrive. I found that most inmates are glad to receive a visit from the chaplain; no doubt it is often a welcome break from the long hours they have to spend in their cells. This is especially true of those in solitary confinement, a separate wing of the prison. Most of these men have asked for 'solitary': many of them are in prison for sexual offences and are afraid of being molested by other inmates.

Lewes Prison is a closed, or maximum security, establishment. It contains not only convicted prisoners, including a number of men sentenced to life imprisonment, but also a large number of men who are on remand or awaiting sentence.

The convicted men, especially the lifers, seem to be looked after best. Each man has a cell to himself and, as they are 'inside' for some time, it is worth while for the prison authorities to take some trouble over them. There are educational classes open to them and instruction in crafts such as woodwork, bricklaying and engineering. Many of the more reliable men have been given special jobs: in the kitchen, or working in the gardens, or cleaning, or helping in the library, or as staff orderlies. They can use the gym and take part in organised open-air sports.

Life is not so interesting for the many men on remand. Often they are cramped: three in a cell which was only intended for one inmate. As they are, in theory, birds of passage, and only in for a short time, it is not considered necessary to arrange educational classes or courses in vocational training for them. But, such are the appalling delays in the English judicial system, many men on remand stay in prison for many months awaiting trial; sometimes over a year.

A considerable number of men at Lewes were West Africans. Some of them were not at all of a criminal class. All too often I would be told the same story: a young man would board a plane at Lagos, in order to visit a relative in London. At Lagos airport he would be approached by a stranger: 'Hi man, do you want to earn a fiver? Here is a small package. If you take it and hand it over to my uncle, who will meet you at the Arrivals gate wearing a rose in his lapel, you will earn the money.' The boy would agree to this, and be picked up at Gatwick for smuggling drugs.

It was a wrong and foolish thing to do, but often the boy concerned would be far from being of a vicious or criminal type. Then for months he would be at Lewes, awaiting trial. Lonely, away from home and friends, in a foreign country with a cold climate and foreign food, these young men would be in the depths of misery. Some of them came from good Christian homes and they were often extremely grateful for the help and friendship offered by the chaplain. They were regular and faithful in worship and provided the majority of our church choir.

Attendance at the Sunday services in the rather beautiful prison chapel was always voluntary; men wishing to attend had to give their names to the prison officers the night before. I realised that the motive for attendance was not always a disinterested hungering for the spiritual life. Often men were glad to get out of their cells and enjoyed the atmosphere and the hymn singing. The form of service was a simple Sung Eucharist and the chaplain had found that the best book to give them was a very simple illustrated missal which had been designed for children but which suited the mental abilities of many of the congregation.

After I had been there some time, I found a nice group of men who wished to be prepared for confirmation. We had weekly confirmation classes for some months and eventually I presented nine candidates for confirmation. As the confirmation service obviously had to be in the prison chapel, I obtained permission for a retired bishop who lived in our parish to conduct the service.

On the morning of the confirmation, one of my candidates, while exercising in the prison yard, had his head cut open by a brick hurled by another inmate: a different kind of laying-on of hands. As he had to miss the service, I was left with one candidate ready but not yet confirmed. I rang up the then Bishop of Lewes, the Right Reverend Peter Ball, who, with his twin brother (now the Bishop of Truro), had founded the Community of the Glorious Ascension, an Anglican religious order which has been much concerned with work amongst young people.

Despite the many calls on his time, Bishop Peter agreed at once to come over and confirm this one prisoner. It was a confirmation I will never forget. At that time the chapel was closed for redecoration, so our service had to be held in a large and bleak reception hall, devoid of all furniture and without any kind of helpful atmosphere. I had arranged a temporary altar but, of course, we had no organ or choir, or any of the usual accompaniments of a big confirmation service. However, the bishop could not have taken more care or trouble over the service. He brought with him great charisma and grace. The service was truly numinous and we all felt we had been brought into the presence of Almighty God.

Although the main responsibility of the Anglican chaplain was to care for the inmates who were members of the Church of England, his duties also included seeing that the spiritual needs of other inmates were met. Roman Catholics and Methodists had their own part-time chaplains, but the Anglican chaplain had to oversee arrangements for those of non-Christian religions.

Once a week a mullah would come by car to conduct a religious service for the Moslems. Sometimes it was part of my duties to bring together the Moslems for this service, collecting them one by one from their cells and taking them to the room allocated for their worship.

The mullah would bring with him a large receptacle containing a savoury mess for a feast after the service. This would be warmed up during the service and then brought in and placed on the floor in the centre of the room. I was often honoured by being invited to this feast. I would sit cross-legged on a blanket on the floor, in a circle with the others. Each would plunge his hand into the glutinous stew and bring out some precious morsel. As an honoured guest, I was given a spoon to scoop out my portion. Sometimes, as a special treat, I would be given a sheep's eye and would do my best to cope with it. Sometimes I reflected that this was an odd way for a retired parson in Sussex to spend his afternoon.

The house in which I am living was given to the diocese of Chichester as a retirement home for clergy and dependants of clergy. It is a substantial stone house, built a century or more ago, standing in large grounds and with spacious lawns facing the downs to the south. The diocese built in the grounds eight bungalows for married couples. In the house the majority of the residents are widows. To outward appearances they may seem a rather dull lot, but I soon found they share wonderful memories of lives spent, often in romantic places, all over the world: British Columbia, South Africa, the Middle East, the Holy Land and many other places. I wonder whether any other profession or calling can show such interesting groups of retired old people.

Since I came here, fifteen years ago, I have had some very interesting holidays. I have never seen the sense of going to travel agents or booking on package tours. When I had my car, it was easy to drive the few miles to Newhaven. At the booking office there I would buy a return passenger's ticket to Dieppe, having left my car at a garage near the station. In Dieppe, I would buy at the ticket office a return ticket to Paris; there is an excellent train service to Paris.

I never troubled to book accommodation beforehand, nor have

I ever found any trouble in securing a room. I much prefer to go and look at a hotel first and would not care for rooms booked in advance by a London travel agent. I have found that there are many small hotels on the Left Bank, offering comfortable accommodation at much cheaper prices than in the centre of Paris. After a feast of art galleries for a day or two, I would then get a return ticket to Chartres, which is only a short way from Paris.

Chartres is one of my spiritual homes. I have been fortunate enough to go there on a number of occasions and never fail to be thrilled and inspired and enchanted by the wonder of the cathedral, with its incomparable stained glass and unforgettable Gothic architecture.

Sometimes I would go on from Chartres to the Benedictine monastery at Solesmes, which is renowned throughout the world for the beauty of its Gregorian plainsong. The abbey at Solesmes is always ready to welcome an Anglican priest who wishes to make a private retreat or spend a few days there in quiet and reading. The monks' friendship and hospitality is typical of the Benedictine tradition.

The year 1982 was, for me, an *annus mirabilis* for holidays. My short forays to Chartres and Solesmes had been made on my own, but for a longer holiday I much prefer to go with a friend. So, in May of that year, I flew to Gibraltar with my old friend Archie Franklin. We have been friends since our undergraduate days. He, like me, is a retired priest. We have had a number of holidays together – often in the Alps, as we both enjoy the same kind of walking holiday.

On this occasion, we stayed for a couple of nights at a comfortable hotel in the main street of Gibraltar, which I found a fascinating place. I hired there a little Fiat car. Having become accustomed to it by driving round the circular road which encircles the colony, the next day we took it on the ferry across to Tangier. We drove on to Rabat, the capital of Morocco, and stayed there a few days. Rabat is a fine city, its wide boulevards bearing witness to its long French occupation. We also enjoyed

exploring the old *medina* (bazaar) and some of the ruined mos-
ques and castles.

From Rabat we drove to Casablanca, a thriving modern city
with bustling crowds and great traffic problems. After a couple
of nights there, we motored to Marrakech. Morocco is a splendid
country for car touring. The roads are almost empty of traffic
but have splendid tarmac surfaces. All the time we were in the
country we had splendid weather, with unbroken blue skies and
very hot, sunny days. I found the Moroccan people very friendly
and helpful. Outside the towns, very few spoke or understood
English but, with my fragmentary schoolboy French, we
managed without any problems.

Marrakech is, of course, a wonderful and unforgettable city.
We treated ourselves rather well and stayed in a fine big luxury
hotel. The hotel had lovely gardens and a superb open-air swimming pool, which we greatly appreciated during a very hot
spell. We enjoyed exploring the old Arab bazaar (*medina*), with
its narrow alleys and curious little shops. But perhaps the most
striking feature of Marrakech is the great open marketplace,
known as the Djemma el Fna which, for eight centuries, has
been the scene of parades, executions and amusements, as well
as of buying and selling of all kinds.

The marketplace is about the size of three or four rugger
pitches. Soon after noon it begins to fill up with a motley crowd
of many nationalities: Moors, Berbers, Africans, Algerians, many
in white robes with turbans, mixing with a scattering of Euro-
pean tourists. There are vendors of every kind of food, grain
merchants and water-sellers, dealers in secondhand goods and
sellers of fruit and vegetables. Every afternoon, snake-charmers,
story-tellers, jugglers, fire-eaters, dancers, musicians and enter-
tainers of every description appear and each is surrounded by
a crowd, large or small according to his power of attraction.
There are open-air restaurants and food stalls in abundance,
with cauldrons full of appetising soup and boiling kettles and
samovars ready for making mint tea, the favourite national
drink.

But the really thrilling time in Marrakech comes with the

going down of the sun. Many of the buildings, and the city walls and gates, are built of reddish-coloured mud and the sunset casts a reddish glow over the whole place. Other walls and buildings are built of ochre-coloured mud, which deepens to a rich golden rose as the sun sinks to the horizon, while the tiled mosaics of many minarets reflect the delicate turquoise tints of the sky with, in the distance, the snowy ramparts of the Atlas Mountains. It is one of the loveliest cities in the world, its beauty only marred by the presence of many beggars and the signs of disease and poverty in their faces.

We had a pleasant drive back to Tangier and our ferry, and left Morocco with many memories of a delightful holiday.

Later that year, in September, I was fortunate enough to have a second overseas holiday. Accompanied by another old friend, I drove my Fiesta to Dover to board the Dover-Calais ferry for a ten-day tour of Belgium, a country I had not visited before and found extremely interesting and worthwhile. From Calais, we drove to Dunkirk to see the famous embarkation beaches. We had a nice swim in a warm sea and it was easy to realise how these wide sands and gradually shelving beach made it possible for so many men to be taken off in small ships.

Our next stop was at Poperinge, a small Flemish town where, in December 1915, the Reverend P B (Tubby) Clayton opened Talbot House as a club (and more) for our troops. So it is the place where the Toc H movement was born, which, after the First World War, grew into a large movement with branches all over the world. The comfortable old house has been preserved and is now used by Toc H members and others as a hostel, many of the visitors coming to tour the battlefields of the First World War.

It was a great privilege for me to celebrate Holy Communion in the Upper Room, a chapel still kept much as it was in those grim war years, with memories of the hundreds of men who made their last communion there before moving up to the trenches. Amongst my small congregation was the Dean of Poperinge (the local RC Priest). This friendly act of brotherhood was typical of the warm welcome I was given by all the Roman Catholics I met in Belgium.

We stayed several days in Poperinge and went on various expeditions. One was to Ypres, where we visited the impressive memorial to those of our dead who have no other memorial – the Menin Gate. At 8 pm we attended the ceremony, which has been held there every evening since the First World War, with the exception of the grim period of German occupation. All traffic is stopped on the busy road and three buglers sound the Last Post, while silence is kept in honour of the British dead. We found this solemn act of remembrance most moving – and thought-provoking, as we considered the many English folk who seem to forget those who made the Supreme Sacrifice.

One day was spent in a longer expedition, via Mons, to a scene of English valour in an earlier war: Waterloo. I had long wanted to see the battlefield of Waterloo. It was thrilling to find the Château d'Hougemont, a lovely old farmhouse, with plaques on the wall commemorating the Guards who defended it so valiantly. The walls of the farmhouse still bear the marks of gunfire sustained during that long siege.

After our stay at Poperinge, we drove to the great Benedictine abbey of Maredsous, not many miles from Brussels. For years I had hoped to make a pilgrimage to Maredsous, the scene of the labours of the famous Abbot Columba Marmion. His books on the spiritual life had helped and inspired countless folk of many denominations and had certainly been a great help to me. The present abbot, a surprisingly young-looking man and a very friendly one, most kindly allowed me to celebrate the Holy Communion at the Altar of St Gregoire, beside the tomb of Abbot Marmion. I was served by my holiday companion, who had been trained by me as a server forty years before, and the abbot was good enough to put at my disposal some vestments and communion vessels.

Greatly to my surprise, after this service the abbot asked me whether I would like to co-celebrate at the Community Sung Mass at the high altar of the great abbey church. I was very moved and honoured at being offered such a privilege. Once again I was robed in the appropriate vestments. The celebrant was one of the older monks and I took my place in the semicircle of co-celebrants. The abbot played the organ and then, later in the morning, gave us copious drinks of whisky before taking us to an excellent lunch in the monastic refectory.

A day or two later we visited another famous Benedictine monastery, having a cross-country drive via the beautiful valley of the Meuse. Our destination this time was the Monastère de la Sainte Croix at Chevetogne. This monastery has earned a worldwide reputation for its studies of the Eastern Orthodox Church. Each day the liturgy is celebrated in the two traditions: Latin and Byzantine. In addition to the small Latin chapel, they have a very beautiful Eastern Orthodox chapel, with an iconostasis and many shrines. We were welcomed by the guest-master, who had the splendid name of Father Christmas, and I noticed that the previous name in the visitors' book was that of His Grace the Right Reverend Robert Runcie, who has taken a special interest in the Eastern Orthodox Church.

After a short visit to Brussels, our next stop was at Bruges. I had long wished to visit this city and now realise why it is considered one of the most beautiful cities in Europe. We loved the many canals, flanked by splendid medieval buildings and crossed by innumerable stone bridges. We strolled in the narrow back streets and hidden alleys, with their cobbles. Almost every building in Bruges is adorned with the traditional Flemish stepped gable roof. We visited the Groeinenge Museum, to wonder at the paintings by Van Eyck, Memling, Bosch and Brueghel the Younger. At the Church of Our Lady we saw the white marble statue of the Madonna carved by Michelangelo. There was so much to see: the splendid baroque church of St Walburga, the Basilica of the Holy Blood, the cathedral and the ancient Gothic town hall.

Each evening we dined at a comfortable, yet quite reasonable, restaurant in the splendid Market Square and saw how much the Belgians appreciated good food.

But perhaps the highlight of our stay was a visit to the Convent of the English Ladies. This very interesting community was founded in Douai at a time when Roman Catholics were being persecuted in England, and was established for English women who wished to enter the religious life under vows. After some years, the community, which follows the Augustinian rule, moved to Bruges. But in the nineteenth century they opened a daughter house at Haywards Heath, Sussex, where, for many years, they ran a successful girls' boarding school. A few years ago, finding, like many other religious communities – both Anglican and Roman – that the qualifications for specialist teaching had become more difficult and that they no longer had enough nuns with suitable qualifications, the school was closed and the community moved to Sayers Common, which is only about four miles from my home.

Here they run a conference centre and retreat house, which is open to members of all denominations and where Anglicans are especially welcome. They had been very kind to me personally and I was charged with a message to the Lady Abbess at Bruges. She was most charming and welcoming and allowed me to celebrate Holy Communion in their chapel, where, once again, I was served by my companion. If only Roman Catholics in this country were allowed to be as friendly and helpful as Belgian Catholics, it would give much added power to the ecumenical movement.

We could easily have spent another week in Bruges, exploring and appreciating its artistic treasures but, as our time was up, the following morning we had to drive off to Ostend for the ferry home.

Perhaps more English folk would visit and tour in Belgium if it was not so near and so little spoken of.

In the fifteen years since I retired, I have also made two visits to Italy, where I returned to one of the Meccas of my life (Florence) and I also flew out to Canada for a fortnight to visit old friends. But life is not all holidays and, in the periods when I was not taking duty as temporary priest-in-charge during a parish interregnum, or helping out while some of my neighbouring priests were ill or on holiday, I took services at Hurstpierpoint parish church. For ten years I acted as honorary assistant priest there. It is a delightful parish, with well attended services and a fine band of layfolk who, with their rector, have made the parish church the focal point of the whole community.

One of the most rewarding experiences of the years since I retired has been my visits to the Anglican Benedictine nuns of Malling Abbey, Kent. This enclosed community has a retreat house where visitors of both sexes are welcome to stay for retreats or for periods of refreshment and contemplation. The abbey is a place of great beauty and historical interest, set in spacious grounds. One cannot fail to be deeply impressed by the quiet and serenity and holiness of Malling Abbey.

I was also surprised and intrigued to discover how closely the community is in touch with the needs and problems of the world outside the convent walls; this is doubtless due to the unceasing flow of requests for the prayers of the community and to the continuous intercessions in their chapel for the needs and sufferings of the world. The Lady Abbess took a great interest in the work I was doing at Lewes Prison and I got into the habit of writing to her when I encountered special problems or difficulties in my ministry there.

Amongst other things, I am grateful to Malling Abbey for curing me of smoking. I had smoked regularly since the age of fifteen and was a twenty-cigarettes-a-day man. But, knowing that the nuns were not keen on tobacco smoke in their guest-house, I stopping smoking for a week and afterwards thought: 'Why start again?'

2
Beaulieu
1960–1977

Ecclesiae Sanctae Mariae de Bello-loco Regis

The name given by King John in 1204, in the charter
which established the Abbey Church of the Blessed
Virgin Mary of Beau Lieu of the King.

I was inducted as vicar of Beaulieu in July 1960 and retired in
July 1977.

Beaulieu must be one of the most unusual and interesting
parishes in the country. When I first went there I found that
practically the entire parish was owned by the Beaulieu Estate:
land, farms, cottages, shops and the Beaulieu river; not only the
banks, but also the bed of the river (which is most unusual in
this country). A few years later some of the outlying parts of
the estate were sold and some leaseholds of larger houses converted into freeholds. The parish is also unusual in that only
once in the last seven hundred and fifty years has the Estate
had a change of ownership.

In the year 1204, King John gave about 8,000 acres of the
New Forest to the Cistercian order to build a monastery. The
Cistercian monks remained there until the suppression of the
monasteries in 1538. King Henry VIII then sold the monastic
buildings and lands to Thomas Wriothesley, First Earl of Southampton. Since then, the Estate has remained in the same family.
The present owner, Lord Montagu of Beaulieu, is a direct
descendant of the First Earl of Southampton, although the succession has not always been in the male line.

Beaulieu is the only one of the many Cistercian foundations
in this country to have been established directly from the mother

house of the order at Citeaux; all the others were founded by daughter houses of Citeaux.

By the year 1246 the monks had completed building the vast abbey church and the great range of monastic buildings. The dedication, on 17 June 1246, was a great occasion, when the church was consecrated in the presence of King Henry III, his wife Eleanor and his son, the future King Edward I. The dedication ceremonies were conducted by the Bishop of Winchester, helped by the bishops of Bath and Wells, Exeter and Chichester, surrounded by a great assembly of notables.

The church was named the Church of the Blessed Virgin Mary of Bellus Locus of the King; the name in French was Beau Lieu (Beautiful Place) and the village which grew up around the monastery became known as Beaulieu (commonly pronounced 'Bewley'). It is astonishing how quickly the monks built the great range of stone buildings: the vast abbey church, the cloisters, the refectory, the chapter house, dormitories for both the monks and lay brothers, the infirmary, kitchens, domestic buildings and the abbot's lodging – or 'Great Gatehouse'.

A circle of granges (or small monasteries) was established in outlying parts of the estate, so that those working on the land need not return each night to the mother house. A huge barn (whose ruins still stand) was built to store the grain and a culvert built to bring clear water from a spring a mile away. This was still supplying the village with water until only a few years ago.

For three hundred and fifty years the quiet, ordered life of worship and work continued. The monks and lay brothers tilled the ground, grew the corn, tended their animals and planted their vineyard. After the Dissolution, the great range of monastic buildings was demolished. The stone was carted away or put on barges on the Beaulieu river. England being then in danger of invasion, it was used to build Hurst Castle, Calshott Castle and two large blockhouses at Cowes.

Fortunately the villagers of Beaulieu managed to save the monks' refectory (dining-hall) for use as a parish church. It has remained the parish church of Beaulieu until today and it makes an exceedingly lovely church: rectangular, without pillars or aisles and covered with a splendid wooden roof. A narrow stone staircase, built in the thickness of the wall, leads up to the lector's pulpit, from which a reader would read from some suitable book while the monks ate their meals in silence. Today it is used as the pulpit of the church.

I shall always remember my first weekend in the parish. Lord Montagu was holding a jazz festival in his grounds next to the abbey. This attracted thousands more people than had been anticipated. On the Saturday evening all the roads leading to Beaulieu were packed with cars and the village was overwhelmed by a great crowd of visitors. In order to find room for parking, some people broke down gates and parked their cars without permission in farmers' fields.

When it became dark some of the crowd became disorderly and set fire to some wooden buildings. The sky was lurid with flames and fire engines arrived from all around, while the programme being broadcast by the BBC was disrupted by drunken brawlers. Extra police had also to be drafted in from all over Hampshire.

Next morning many local householders found that their fences had been broken down for firewood and their lawns used as lavatories. The church porch had to be swept clear of used and discarded condoms.

The meadow next to my vicarage was full of parked cars and people dossing down for the night. On Sunday morning I had a queue of people at the vicarage door, asking for water or for permission to use the lavatory. It took some time to clear the village and surrounding fields of broken glass and litter. However successful the festival was from the point of view of jazz lovers, the villagers and residents of Beaulieu were, to say the least, unenthusiastic.

When, the following year, Lord Montagu organised another jazz festival, I felt that, with so many thousands coming for the weekend, I ought to arrange an open-air service for the visitors on the Sunday in the ruins of the abbey. With the help and cooperation of Lord Montagu, this was organised and attended by several hundred people. I invited an Anglican Franciscan to give the address and the hymns were accompanied by Johnny Dankworth and his band, Cleo Laine helping with the singing.

Once again the roads were blocked by traffic. Johnny Dankworth and his band had been put up at hotels in Southampton and, owing to the traffic jams, they arrived late and the service started, with the musicians gradually arriving, one by one. Fortunately for the village, not long after this, jazz festivals at Beaulieu came to an end. It was rumoured that this was due to an empty beer bottle having been thrown through the windows of the nursery in His Lordship's house.

Beaulieu has, of course, become known far and wide because of the motor museum. Soon after he came into his heritage, on his twenty-fifth birthday in 1952, Lord Montagu began forming the motor museum as a tribute to his father, the Second Lord Montagu of Beaulieu, who had been a leading pioneer of motoring in this country. It began in a small way, with a few exhibits in the entrance hall of his home, Palace House, which was open to visitors.

It became very popular and so further exhibits were acquired and new premises built to contain them, near to the house. Within ten years, by his energy and business acumen, Lord Montagu had raised his Montagu Motor Museum to the position of the foremost exhibition of its kind in Europe. By the 1960s the museum was attracting 500,000 visitors a year. This huge influx into an unspoiled little village created considerable problems for the residents, traffic conditions often being in a state of complete chaos.

It was a relief to everyone when, in the 1970s, new and much larger premises were built, fortunately further away from the village and the abbey, with adequate parking and better access roads. Now known as the National Motor Museum, it is one of the country's foremost tourist attractions.

Until after the Second World War, Beaulieu was a very quiet

village indeed, with little traffic apart from a steady stream of visitors who came to see the impressive ruins of the abbey.

It had a somewhat unbalanced population of either very rich people or cottagers and estate workers. The Second Lord Montagu had granted leaseholds for about thirty large and luxurious houses, many occupied in the first place by his own personal friends. Apart from a handful of farmers and shopkeepers, there were hardly any middle-class people such as teachers, doctors, solicitors, office workers or executives, as there was nowhere for them to live. People like this are often staunch supporters of the church and ready to use their gifts in its service.

By the time I came to Beaulieu, many occupiers of the big houses were Londoners, who only came down at weekends and took little interest in the village or the church.

Fortunately the position was saved by the fact that a number of people came to our church from outside the parish; some were originally Beaulieu folk who had been unable to obtain homes in the parish; some were drawn by the beauty of the church and others came because they could not endure the 'Low Church' ethos of their own parish.

It is one of the sorrows of the Church of England that the patronage of many parishes has been acquired by narrow and partisan party trusts (mainly evangelical) who have clamped on the unfortunate parishes they control an outdated form of churchmanship, irrespective of the needs or desires of parishioners, bishops or anyone else.

When I retired, in 1977, the parish in the previous ninety years had only had the experience of having a married vicar for eight years. This was partly due to the very long incumbency of my illustrious predecessor, the Reverend R F Powles, who came to the parish as assistant curate in 1880, was appointed vicar in 1886 and retired (under protest) in 1939, having ministered for fifty-nine years in the parish. After Father Powles, there were five vicars in thirty-seven years!

Robert Frazer Powles was in every way a most remarkable man. He was tall, handsome, well-built and, in his younger

The 'Abbot': the Reverend R F Powles
(Vicar of Beaulieu Abbey Church, 1886–1939)

days, had been quite an athlete. He was unmarried and for many years he did his own washing and made his own butter; at one period he milked his own cows. On Sundays he wore black serge, but on weekdays he wore a suit of cream serge, similar in colour and texture to the habits of Cistercian monks. He wore a wide-brimmed white or grey hat, with white or grey spats to complete his attire. He carried a heavy ebony stick with a large silver head. It was his custom to walk up the village street in the middle of the road, there being little traffic in those days; indeed, all the roads leading into Beaulieu had wooden gates across them.

He was regarded by the villagers, if not as a god, then as the uncrowned king of Beaulieu. He had not only baptised and married most of his parishioners, but had done the same also for most of their parents.

For his time, he had quite a good standard of churchmanship. Matins and Evensong were said every day and the Angelus was rung each evening. Despite living at a time of strict sabbatarianism, he encouraged his choirboys to play cricket or football on Sunday afternoons, in the church meadow, and sometimes played with them. He organised dances and parish parties for the villagers, which were a great success. Long before it became the custom, he encouraged the children of the village school to attend Holy Communion, in order to familiarise them with the service before their confirmation. For this he was sternly rebuked by his patron, Lord John, and there followed a most interesting three-cornered correspondence between Lord Montagu, Father Powles and the Archbishop of Canterbury, Randall Davidson, who had been drawn into the dispute. Father Powles stood his ground and was eventually vindicated by the archbishop, so peace was restored. In support of his pastoral methods, the vicar mentioned to the archbishop (in one of his letters) that, at Easter, out of an adult population of 520 there were 300 communicants.

Until 1939 the parish of Beaulieu was a donative, ie it was exempt from episcopal jurisdiction and did not come under the authority of the bishop of Winchester. In 1892 the Benefices Act was passed, which abolished donatives but, as it did not come into effect in the lifetime of existing incumbents, Beaulieu remained a donative until 1939. The Estate paid the parson and the clerk and the organist, provided a house for the vicar to live in and bore much of the cost of the maintenance and repair of the church.

At various times down the centuries, the diocese endeavoured to gain greater control. In the eighteenth century an attempt was made by the Archdeacon of Southampton to conduct a visitation of the parish. The then Lord of the Manor (the Duke of Montagu) replied, saying that if the archdeacon came the duke and his men would throw him into the water. The archdeacon made the diplomatic reply: 'I have received the letter from your grace, and have decided not to come to Beaulieu as I do not want to experience such a reception as would be fitting neither for you to give nor me to receive.'

Although free from diocesan supervision and control, Vicar Powles was devoted to Winchester cathedral and, for many years, took his confirmation candidates there to be confirmed, conveying them by wagon and horse or by coach. In his later years, when Bishop Garbett had become bishop of Winchester, he often visited Beaulieu in the course of his annual walking tour and peregrination of the diocese. He doubtless regarded the old man as a great character and humoured his eccentricities; at any rate, they became firm friends.

Father Powles regarded himself as the successor to the mitred abbots of Beaulieu and one of his endearing ploys was to have made for himself a mitre. He wore this on special occasions, with a magnificent cope which the parish is still proud to possess. When the bishop came to services in Beaulieu church, he was not suffered to walk last in the procession (as is normally the custom) but the bishop and the vicar would process down the aisle side by side, both coped and mitred.

Before the days of the Enabling Act of 1919, there were no parochial church councils. The functions they now perform were previously exercised by the churchwardens and vestry. An annual vestry meeting was held, when churchwardens and sidesmen were elected, the accounts passed and necessary business transacted. Father Powles had his own inimitable way of dealing with vestry meetings. For many years during his long reign, the records show that only the vicar and the clerk attended the meetings. Very occasionally another person came and, on even rarer occasions, there were two other people there. Even when only the vicar and the clerk attended, all the necessary resolutions were duly proposed and seconded and the minutes record that they were carried unanimously which, in the circumstances, was not surprising.

After his resignation in 1939, for the first time a parochial church council for Beaulieu came into existence. One of its first tasks was to send a letter to the bishop and to the patron describing the kind of man the parish needed and the attributes required. After some discussion, the PCC felt that, if possible, the new parson should have all seven of the following qualifications:

1 Be aged 35–50,
2 Preferably married,
3 A man keen on visiting,
4 Good with the young and boys,
5 Small private income, if possible,
6 Continue the type of service as in the past, unless otherwise desired by the parish,
7 A good preacher.

Some twenty years later, during the vacancy which preceded my appointment, a later PCC faced the same daunting task. It was decided to send a resolution to the bishop and to the patron, with a list practically the same as the earlier one.

At the next meeting of the council, which was held after I had arrived and over which I presided, the minutes of the previous meeting were duly read out. The members of the PCC looked very embarrassed as the list was read, while I found it difficult to keep a straight face. Before signing the minutes, I said, 'Dear members of the PCC, I am extremely sorry that you do not seem to have got any of the things that you asked for; however, I will do my best to serve you.'

Towards the end of his life, the old vicar became very infirm and unsteady at the altar. The churchwardens became concerned. However, the Reverend P B Clayton (founder of Toc H and vicar of All Hallows by the Tower), who had long been devoted to the old man, used to send down one of his curates or Toc H padres each week. Amongst those who came were Pat Leonard, Tom Savage and Cuthbert Bardsley, all of whom became bishops later on. The parents of 'Tubby' Clayton had had a holiday home near Hatchett Pond, in the parish. Older residents remembered Tubby as an undergraduate, swimming in the pond while smoking a pipe, managing to keep the bowl above the water.

When the aged vicar was eventually persuaded to resign, he would not move out of the house which served as a vicarage and in which he had lived so long. The dear old man died there during the darkest days of the war, in 1942, at the age of ninety-six. Meanwhile the parish managed to rent a cottage from the Estate to house the new vicar, the Reverend Cyril Pearson, who, fortunately, was unmarried.

After I had been in the parish five years, I thought it was time that we had a parish Mission. The previous one (and the only one on record) had been held in 1886. I invited the Society of St Francis, the Anglican friars from Dorset, to conduct the Mission, for which we prepared carefully. They sent Brother Simon and Brother William, together with a novice and a woman helper.

Brother Simon and Brother William were young, attractive and well suited to their work. The woman helper was Mrs Wilkes, whose husband had been warden of Radley College and had left it to minister in a working-class parish near Leeds. The fact that she was a sister of the Earl of Home, recently Prime Minister of England, no doubt added prestige to the Mission in the eyes of some of my parishioners and she did splendid work amongst the women. Simon had been educated at Harrow and had been a Guards officer before joining the Franciscans. Brother William was very musical and had composed a number of hymns in a light-music style, which he sang, accompanying himself on the guitar.

The Mission lasted a fortnight and made a deep impression on the parish. It was not so much what the Missioners said, but what they were, that counted. The fact that these young men had, for Christ's sake and the Gospel, taken life vows of poverty, chastity and obedience, was a great challenge to the somewhat self-indulgent lives of some of our parishioners. Once again it became clear to me that members of the religious orders and communities in the Church of England exercised a far greater influence and importance than their numbers would suggest.

Shortly after the Mission, Brother Simon and Brother William flew to Brisbane to open the first house of Anglican Franciscans in Australia. After a few years, Brother Simon was, alas, killed in a climbing accident in the Australian mountains. By September 1991, the Society of St Francis had established three houses in Australia, one in New Zealand, three in Papua New Guinea and four in the Solomon Islands. Their numbers had grown to forty friars and thirty-three novices. So the small seeds sown by Brothers Simon and William had grown wonderfully. As in the early days of Christianity, 'the blood of the martyrs was the seed of the Church'.

For me, personally, the period of the Mission was a very difficult time, owing to an unexpected death at the vicarage. My mother had come to live with me, accompanied by an old family friend who acted as her companion. The friend died suddenly from a heart attack. Not long afterwards I became ill and overstrained and my doctor insisted that I should go away for a few weeks.

As it was midwinter, I was somewhat perplexed as to where to go, until I remembered an invitation from the parents of one of my old boys at Bryanston School; to stay with them on their farm in Kenya. I cabled them and, quite soon, was on a plane bound for Nairobi.

My ticket allowed me to break my journey so, on the way

out, I spent a few days in Rome, which I had not visited before and, amongst other experiences, was given an invitation to a combined Audience by the Pope.

I also stayed for a week at Addis Ababa, where an old friend of mine had been made headmaster of a school for the sons of Ethiopian chiefs – the General Wingate School – which was run by English public school methods. I found my stay with him was fascinating, especially because while I was there I attended, in the Orthodox cathedral at Addis Ababa, a Memorial Service for Winston Churchill, who had just died. It was an impressive occasion, attended by King Haile Selassie and his consort and the heads of all the diplomatic missions and legations, robed in full regalia. Outside the cathedral, the Guards of the royal bodyguard were lined up. They were dressed just like our Guards, with busbies and thick red tunics which, in the tropical temperature and burning sun, must have been most uncomfortable.

Another memorable occasion during my stay in Addis Ababa was a State Visit by our Queen and Prince Philip. I stood loyally in the crowd as their procession passed by, together with the thousands of black spectators who were jammed together round me, waving a welcome.

I found Addis Ababa fascinating. The big powers of Europe and Asia were jostling for favours in Ethiopia and, in order to curry favour, were putting up dazzling new buildings of concrete and glass for hospitals, schools, libraries and cultural centres. Apart from these and the royal palace, most of the buildings were built of wood, with corrugated iron roofs. There was not one public convenience in the city, but the inhabitants found that the gardens in the central square were quite convenient. At night, hyenas could be heard roaring in the surrounding countryside.

My friends in Kenya lived sixty miles from Nairobi, at Makuyu, running a farm for growing coffee and tobacco. It was not long after the Mau Mau times and their farm had been in the middle of the troubles. I was greatly impressed by the stories I was told by some of their neighbours. Amongst them were widows living alone who had remained on their farms all through the uprising, sleeping at night with rifles by their pillows.

During my visit I spent a night at the well-known Treetops Hotel, where our Queen had been staying when she first heard of the death of King George VI. We stayed up most of the night, watching the wild beasts creep onto the floodlit salt lick, rather like actors taking their turn on the stage. We saw elephants, rhinos, buffalos and waterbucks. Meanwhile we had to fend off the marauding baboons, who swung down and tried to steal our refreshments as we sat on the wooden balcony.

After a very refreshing stay with my friends, I returned home from Nairobi airport, again breaking my journey, this time at Athens. Here, for all too short a time, I was able to explore the Acropolis and other wonders, sitting out in the wintry sun, which was all the more enjoyable as there were so few visitors about.

After I had been at Beaulieu for ten years, I was given a sabbatical: I exchanged places with the chaplain of the Episcopal Hospital at Philadelphia. He came, with his wife and two children, and stayed in my vicarage for six weeks, looking after our parish. I stayed in his flat outside Philadelphia and undertook his duties at the hospital, which had originally been founded by the Episcopal Church of America.

Like many Englishmen, I suppose, many of my ideas about American life had been formed from watching American films, with their views of spacious homes and well-tended lawns. I was both surprised and appalled at the poverty and squalor I found in the slum streets surrounding the hospital, which was in the poorest part of the city. England in the 1960s was still reasonably free from violent crime, so I was quite unprepared for the violence and gang warfare which went on round the hospital. Most days men were brought into the casualty wards suffering from stabbing or gun wounds suffered in the streets.

I was also very surprised and disappointed at the ugliness which one found when motoring outside the city. Mile after mile of the roads were lined by advertising hoardings, gas stations, shabby motels, quick-food bars and squalid little shacks and hotels. I am sure America must have some lovely countryside, but I never found it. Although I am not a lover of government restrictions, I felt America had a lot to learn from our planning laws and preservation of the countryside from urban sprawl.

During my stay in Philadelphia, I managed a very short visit to New York. Then, after a month, I was driven by friends six hundred miles (in one day) to their holiday home at Lake Muskoka, Canada.

Lake Muskoka is a large lake about seventy miles north-west of Toronto. It contains about forty small islands, each about big enough for one or two large country houses with surrounding grounds. Most of these are used as holiday homes by the same families that have owned them for generations; often they are business folk from Toronto or American cities like Detroit. Frequently they own small seaplanes and fly up for the weekends, alighting on the lake. They all have motorboats and there is a very active social life, with much inter-island visiting and hospitality.

My host was a delightful American doctor who I had prepared for confirmation thirty years before, when he was a schoolboy at Chillon College, Montreux. His mother, also an old friend of mine, was still alive and, with his hospitable wife and friendly children, we had a delightful holiday; swimming, boating and playing tennis. I returned to Beaulieu, much refreshed, after six weeks in North America.

Apart from these major expeditions, during the seventeen years I was at Beaulieu I was fortunate enough to have three or four walking holidays in the Alps, with Zermatt or Saas Fee as my centre. A friend and I also had holidays at various times at Annecy, Champery, Engelberg and Kitzbühel. But, towards the end of this period, the cost of living in Switzerland became too expensive for English parsons on a low budget. Fortunately, some years before, I had discovered Macugnaga, a delightful Italian alpine village just underneath Monte Rosa on the south side. From it we could have much the same mountain walks and thrilling views as from Zermatt. But the cost of living was about half.

We used to go by train through the Simplon Tunnel and get out at Domodossola, the first stop on the Italian side. From there, we took a rackety little bus for two hours up the Val Anzasca. This is the most thrilling bus journey I have ever taken. The road had innumerable twists and turns, having been hewn out of the mountainside high above the river gorge, often with only a low parapet lining the road. Frequently the road went through tunnels cut out of the rock. The driver tore through these at a frightening speed, frequently sounding his horn and doubtless hoping all would be well. There are several villages perched on the mountainside and the bus was full of a cheerful, talkative crowd of Italian peasants.

Staffa is the central village of a group of four known as Macugnaga. We stayed at the Albergo Nuovo at Pecetto, which is the last village up the valley and the terminus for the bus. It was a small inn with comfortable bedrooms and good food and the charges were very reasonable. I have not been there since 1978, but at that time the valley was still unspoiled.

The valley had originally been colonised from Saas, on the Swiss side of the alps, so the villagers were German-speaking and some still spoke German when we first went there. But after 1918 only Italian was taught in the schools and Italian place names were painted over the old German ones.

The old rhythm of life went on, much as it had done for centuries, and was practically the same as could be seen in the Saas Valley or the Val d'Annivier in Switzerland. Old women, dressed in black with, perhaps, a red head-shawl, would scythe by hand all day in their little strips of smallholding, then carry the hay in great baskets on their backs and climb the steps up the wooden *mayens*, where it would be stored, to feed their cattle in winter.

Pecetto still retained the air of a frontier town (as seen in American Westerns) and, indeed, in a sense it was: just a few wooden chalets, with two hotels and a little ancient church.

Beyond it was a few hundred metres of grass alp, with the fir trees thinning out, then acres of rocky moraine, washed down by the mountain torrents, and ahead the vast amphitheatre formed by the snowy precipices of Monte Rosa and the surrounding mountains. These mountain holidays were a wonderful relaxation from parish life.

During my seventeen years as vicar of Beaulieu, I was given splendid help and support from my churchwardens. One was the mother of Lord Montagu. In 1920, Miss Pearl Barrington Crake was married to John, Second Lord Montagu of Beaulieu. Their marriage was blessed with the birth of three daughters and Edward, the present Earl. Lord John, who was a widower, was considerably older than his young bride. He died in 1929 and, in 1936, Lady Montagu married again, her second husband being Commander, the Honourable Edward Pleydell-Bouverie, brother of the Earl of Radnor. They had one son. Commander Pleydell-Bouverie was a serving naval officer, away for much of the year. He died in 1951.

Pearl Pleydell-Bouverie became a church warden in 1929 and, having been re-elected in every year since, she is still in office at the time of writing. She is a remarkable and outstanding woman, the mother of five children, now with many grandchildren and an innumerable brood of great-grandchildren. She has a great love of family and often has huge family parties in the dower house, The Lodge, which is now her home.

From 1929 until the present Lord Montagu took over the Estate in 1951, she reigned over Beaulieu manor with, for much of the time, the help of Captain H E Widnell, the Estate agent. She knew everyone in the village – and the names of all the children.

Possessed with immense energy, for sixty years she has taken the lead in every conceivable local activity: as commodore of the Beaulieu River Sailing Club, president or chairman of local branches of innumerable societies (such as the Red Cross, the Royal British Legion and the Lifeboat Society), chairman of the managers of Beaulieu School and, besides these village activities, she takes an important part in county affairs. Above all, she has been devoted to Beaulieu Abbey church and unswerving in her support of it. She is admired and loved by all who know her and it is impossible to think of Beaulieu without her.

When I first came to Beaulieu, the other churchwarden was Captain H E Widnell. He, too, became my very good friend. During the First World War he served in the Seaforth Highlanders, retiring in 1918 on account of a severe head wound. Later in 1918, he was appointed as land agent to John, Second Lord Montagu, and retained this position until his retirement in 1953. Edward, the present Lord Montagu, then appointed him archivist in the Estate Muniment Room, where he worked for another twenty years. During this time he wrote *The Beaulieu Record*, a most interesting (but bulky) book of 511 pages, which was published after another hand had sub-edited it and reduced it to half its previous length. I am indebted to his book for many details concerning Father Powles.

In his early days Captain Widnell was somewhat of a martinet, but he mellowed as he got older. He was a widower when I knew him and lived alone with a rather miserable little dog, to which he was devoted. Blessed with a prodigious memory, he could recite by heart (or sing) the lyrics of nearly all the Gilbert and Sullivan operas. One of his endearing habits was to leave up, hanging on lines in his study, the many Christmas cards he received, until they were taken down in June or July. He was completely straight and honest, greatly respected and admired by all who knew him, who saw in him a perfect example of an English gentleman of the old type.

The village of Beaulieu had long been the home of a number of retired service officers. Indeed, when I first came and when Matins was still in place as the major service, the rota for readers of the lessons read rather like the Army List, with a few naval additions. The four or five Sundays each month were shared by a vice-admiral, a major-general, a colonel, a major and a commodore. Many of these, with their families, gave staunch support to the church.

Vice-Admiral Sir Ballin Robertshaw had been in command of a cruiser in the Pacific at the end of the war with Japan. Foreseeing that they would have to remain on station for some time with little to do, he had had the foresight to lay in a supply of materials for spare-time activities. He would, himself, sit on the deck, embroidering a tapestry. At first the crew, looking at him from a discreet distance, would sneer or jeer. But, when they saw the excellent work he turned out, many of them began embroidering cushions and chair-backs to take home to their wives! One of his tasks at Beaulieu was to organise the embroidering of a number of hassocks for our church and he embroidered several kneelers himself. One of his team of embroiderers was Major-General Ian Macdougall, who worked the emblem of his old regiment, the Scots Greys, on his kneeler.

In an earlier era there had been a splendid old soldier living in Beaulieu, one Colonel Jerrard. At the outbreak of the war in 1914, his first thought was to send his sword to be sharpened. He was most annoyed that the War Office would not accept him for active service, but he was to some extent mollified when he was made a member of the local selection board and he tried to pack off into the services (preferably the army) every farm worker and other essential civilian workers.

During my time in the parish, the church was much strengthened when General (later Sir) Hugh Beech and his wife moved into the parish. The sermons which he gave us were deeply appreciated.

There were several millionaires with houses or holiday homes in the parish. Two of them, brothers, were members of the Showering family: one lived in a delightful house on the Beaulieu river, the other in a house on the shore of the Solent, facing the Isle of Wight. The Showering family had owned some small orchards for cider apples and perry in the Shepton Mallet area. They had made their fortune largely through very clever advertising. The perry drink was put in small bottles with a pretty label. The label had a drawing of a baby chamois and the drink was called Babycham; perhaps some people thought they were buying a small bottle of champagne. Ralph Showering once said to me:

'We think we are fulfilling a public service. The young man who takes out his girl for a pillion ride on his motor-bike often stops for a drink in a pub on the way home. He has a beer and orders a Babycham for his girl. She is pleased because it is a nice fizzy drink and she may feel it is like drinking champagne. He is pleased because it does not cost too much. We are pleased because we make a reasonable profit on the bottle. So everyone is happy.'

But most of my work was with the villagers and farm workers. I could not do much about the thousands of visitors to the motor museum, who came and went rather as the tide ebbs and flows. But I had the largest (in area) parish in Hampshire, which, when I first went there, contained twenty-two farms.

I was very sad to resign as vicar of Beaulieu, as I had been very happy there, had made many good friends and had been given loyal support. But I was aged seventy-one and getting very stale, so I knew it was right for the parish that I should go. My last service was a combined service for the whole parish, appointed to commemorate the Silver Jubilee of the Queen's reign. The happiness of this day came as some mitigation for leaving.

It had been a considerable problem for me to know what to do or where to go when I retired. In most professions, when a man retires he loses his job and probably his business friends and colleagues. But when a priest retires, he not only loses his job but also his home and, as it is nearly always a mistake after retirement to live near one's old parish, he loses also the friends he has made during his incumbency.

After considerable thought, as I did not have enough money to buy a retirement bungalow or cottage, I applied for a bedsitting-room in a Church of England Pensions' Board retirement home. I was offered, and I accepted, a room in their home at Worthing. As I would only have one small room, it meant selling most of my furniture and personal possessions. But what hurt me most of all was selling my library as, over the years, I had collected several hundred books, which I loved.

I moved to Worthing in July 1977 and, for the next six months, spent one of the most unhappy periods in my life. There were so many things I missed: the pleasure of walking out and knowing, and being known by, everyone I met; the interest of going in and out of the homes of my parishioners, cottages, farmhouses and big houses; the friendship of so many people, young and old; the privilege of having watched babies and young children grow up into young men and women; the frequent visits to our village school, of which I was a manager and where I gave a weekly class; the intimate contacts with individuals and families, at times both sad and glad; illness, bereavement, christenings and weddings.

I missed the vicarage, with its spacious sunny rooms, its sitting-room warmed by a large log fire in winter, its garden with lawns and rose beds and a south-facing wall covered with wisteria. I missed the abbey church, where God had been honoured for seven hundred and fifty years, and I longed for the peace and beauty of the cloisters and monastic ruins which had surrounded it. Especially, I missed the parish Eucharist, which I had established as the principal Sunday service and which I had built up over the years.

Worthing seemed to me a very dull place, a town without a soul. Our clergy retirement home was surrounded by private hospitals, nursing homes, homes for the disabled and blind and retirement hostels for the aged. Day after day one heard the sirens of ambulances taking the sick to hospital or the dead to the mortuary. My own room was small and dark and had no view. The house was near the sea-front, but few things are more depressing than a seaside promenade out of season.

Fortunately, after six months I heard of a vacancy at my present home, ten miles from Worthing and on the north side of the downs. This is a much smaller house, more of a home than an institution, and was given to the diocese of Chichester as a retirement home for clergy and their dependants. It is in the country, about a mile and a half from Henfield.

This is a large village. Unlike Worthing, it does not consist mainly of elderly people, but is a mixed community, with plenty of young families and children. The people have varied occupations: some commute to London, Crawley or Brighton; others work on the land, at smallholdings, fruit orchards, farms and riding establishments. This makes for a lively and active community and I have found Henfield a very friendly and interesting village, with an astonishingly varied range of activities.

3
Bryanston
1949–1960

Et Nova et Vetera

From the arms of Bryanston School, taken from
Matthew 13.52:
. . . a man that is an householder, which bringeth
forth out of his treasure things new and old.

In January 1949 I took up my duties as chaplain of Bryanston
School, in Dorset, and remained there for twelve years.

I can never understand why I was appointed: I had not,
myself, been educated at a public school; I did not possess a
good degree; I had never had any teaching experience. But, not
long before my appointment, there had been a Mission at the
school, conducted by Father Algy of the Society of St Francis,
assisted by his young secretary, Brother Michael (who, years
later, became bishop of St German's and subsequently the minister general of the SSF). My predecessor, the Reverend Jack
Winslow, had just resigned and the headmaster of Bryanston
asked Father Algy if he could suggest someone to come as
chaplain. One of my friends, who was a Franciscan, knew that
I had had considerable experience of work with young people,
so my name was suggested.

Bryanston had a twin school for girls, Cranborne Chase
School, then at Witchampton in Dorset, and the appointment
was for a priest to be chaplain at both schools, spending five
days a week at Bryanston and two at the girls' school, which
was smaller. I was interviewed by Mr T F Coade, the headmaster,
and Miss Galton, head of Cranborne Chase. The fact that I had
previously been chaplain of two excellent English girls' schools
established in Switzerland (St George's at Clarens and Chatelard

School at Les Avants) and the help I was given by letters of recommendation from the heads of both these schools probably influenced Mr Coade and Miss Galton in asking me to come.

Bryanston School was one of the newer public schools, having been founded in 1928. The founder was the Reverend Graham Jeffreys, an Australian who graduated at Oxford. Shortly before taking his finals, he was asked what he was going to do when he went down. He replied: 'I am going to found a public school,' and, before many years, this is what he did.

Jeffreys admired much in the traditional public school system, but he thought in some ways it had become too narrow and restrictive and too resistant to new developments in education and to wider interests. The school motto *Et Nova et Vetera* (Things New and Old) summarises his objectives. He gained the support of Dorset notables, such as the Earl of Shaftesbury, and other leading figures in the county and, with their backing, obtained a large loan from an insurance company. With this he bought Bryanston House and several hundred acres of its estate, on the banks of the Stour near to Blandford.

Bryanston was one of the last really big country houses to be built in this country. It was built by Lord and Lady Portman, who pulled down their old home near the river in the 1890s and engaged Norman Shaw, the eminent architect, to build them a new one. Lord and Lady Portman lived there in reasonable comfort, being waited on by an indoor staff of ninety servants. Those were the days when weekend parties with twenty or thirty guests were held frequently and, as each guest might bring a valet or lady's maid, a large staff was needed to look after them all. The many bedrooms all had open fireplaces, so there was much carrying of scuttles of coal upstairs and laying of fires.

But after the First World War they could no longer live in this style and the estate was put up for sale. The building made a splendid home for a school, its parquet flooring and rooms, with their heavy mahogany doors, standing up well to the onslaught of generations of boys.

The school began in 1928, with a small handful of boys. But

soon numbers began to grow. After four years the founder had a dispute with his board of governors and resigned. They appointed, to succeed him, T F Coade, who became headmaster in 1932, at the age of thirty-six. Although he was not the founder, it was Thorold Coade who, in the course of the next twenty-seven years, built up the school and made it one of the leading public schools in the country.

Thorold Coade was a remarkable man and an outstanding head-master. He was given the unswerving loyalty of governors, staff, parents and boys. The son of an Anglican vicar, he was educated at Harrow and in 1915, aged eighteen, went to the Royal Military College at Sandhurst. He was wounded in the Battle of the Somme in 1916. After he was demobilised, in 1918, he went to Christchurch, Oxford. In 1922 he was married and returned to Harrow as an assistant master.

Like some other men of his generation, the fact that, although so many of his closest friends were killed in the war, his own life was spared – and spared in circumstances which he felt were miraculous, gave his life a strong sense of purpose and dedication.

He was a shy and reserved man, with a complex character, and was not very good at meeting strangers. Boys watched the rather diffident figure ambling along the main corridor in a vague kind of way and some may have wondered if he knew what was going on. But those half-closed eyes took it all in. He had a deep compassion and could enter sympathetically into the hearts and minds of many boys, especially difficult ones. Nothing would be too much trouble to help a boy in distress and he would spend hours over one delinquent.

His wife recounted how one day he greeted a boy, as he neared the school after a long walk, with: 'You look tired. What have you got there?' The boy opened his hands and showed a small animal that he had caught. The headmaster asked what he would feed the little creature on and was told worms. Not long afterwards they met in the lower corridor and the head-master put his hand into his jacket pocket and pulled out several fat wriggling worms. 'I have been saving these for you,' he said.

Thorold Coade took a passionate interest in school plays and believed that the team effort involved (ie the skills of actors, stage-hands, scenery painters, electricians and other workers) was, in itself, an excellent educational exercise. He produced many plays himself, his outstanding production probably being that of the Chester Mystery Plays, with a cast of over a hundred.

In his sermons, and in his daily life, he gave expression to the strength of his own Christian faith. After his death some of his sermons were printed. If it was possible for one sentence to summarise his outlook, here is one from an address he gave on 'A New Parable':

> The man who refuses to believe that the Spirit of God, ie the Spirit of Love, was embodied in Jesus, and is waiting patiently to enter and be embodied in himself, though he may pile up for himself possessions and worldly experience, though he may postpone the death of the body, is inviting, every time he shuts the door against the Spirit of Love, the death of the soul.

Under his leadership, Bryanston was a pioneer in new educational ideas. Many of the customs he introduced were scoffed at as ultra-progressive by conventional folk, but they are standard practice in many boarding schools today, eg recognition of the value of the individual, each boy having his own tutor and sometimes his own syllabus; greater provision for music and drama, art and sculpture; opportunities for practising a wide variety of hobbies; the abolition of corporal punishment.

Some critics, who had never been to Bryanston, said: 'That is the school where boys do what they like.' Coade would have replied that boys went to Bryanston to learn to like what they did – and to do it as excellently as possible. It is recounted that he once (with a twinkle in his eye) said to prospective parents, who had asked him foolish 'progressive' questions: 'Bryanston is not a school where the parents run nude amongst the begonias.'

Those who were admitted to his family circle (Thorold and Kathleen Coade had two daughters) found there not only a warm welcome, but much fun and a delicious sense of humour. Kathleen Coade was a wonderful help and support to her husband and also had quite a ministry of her own; in welding into one family the wives and children of the staff. The headmaster had great confidence in his staff and never pried into what they were doing. To give one example of this, he never told me what my duties were, or instructed me in how to do them.

When I began my work, it was obviously important to know, and to be known by, as many of the community as possible. So I began, and continued, the practice of attending all school matches (rugby, cricket and hockey), of going to athletics meetings and of watching the crews practising on the river. Also, I watched as many inter-house games as possible and always went to school concerts, orchestral performances and plays. Sometimes, in the afternoons, I was able to have a game of tennis or squash, my opponents being either other members of the staff or one of the less brilliant players amongst the senior boys.

Pioneering was a great institution at Bryanston. Every boy had to spend at least one afternoon a week in work on the estate. This might involve road-making, forestry, gardening, building construction or farm work. Each gang was in the charge of one member of the staff. Usually I took a group with felling axes for forestry. This was a far better way of getting to know boys than in the classroom.

Compared with most of the teaching staff, I had a very light teaching programme. The headmaster had made it clear that he did not want so much a teacher in Holy Orders as a pastor to the boys, the staff and their families. He would, no doubt, have agreed with the Admiralty, who defined the work of a chaplain as to be the 'friend and advisor of all on board'.

One of my tasks, in consultation with the headmaster, was to invite visiting preachers. These would often be heads of other schools. We had some extremely interesting visitors, including Bishop Trevor Huddleston and Bishop Wilson of Birmingham, who had a son at the school. Bishop Wilson had been bishop of Singapore and thrilled the boys as he told of his experience as a prisoner-of-war, of being tortured and of his joy in baptising some of his torturers after the war.

The sermon I remember best was given by Bishop Walter Carey, retired bishop of Bloemfontein. It is usually considered unwise for a sermon to a school congregation to go on for longer than fifteen minutes. After Bishop Carey had gone on for forty-five minutes I was getting extremely worried, as I realised that the timetables and programmes of many people were being disrupted. While he paused for breath between two sentences, I stood up in my stall and said, 'While the bishop is ending his address, we will prepare to sing the last hymn, number 545.'

Bishop Walter turned round and said, 'Who is giving this sermon? Am I, or is Kenneth Jarvis?' – after which he went on for another ten minutes. I was very concerned at the effect this might have on the boys but I need not have worried, for they loved it. Afterwards, a group of prefects sat at his feet in the headmaster's study. The fact that he had boxed and played rugby for Oxford may have played a part in their respect for him.

Perhaps my main contribution to the life of the school consisted of listening. I had a bedsitting room in the centre of the school and most evenings it was open for callers. There were few days without someone coming in. One of the biggest problems was the large number of boys who came from broken homes. Sometimes at the beginning of term I would greet boys coming back from the holidays and say, 'Have you had a good vac?'

Often they would reply: 'No. I have had a lousy time. I spent a fortnight with Mother and then a fortnight with Father. Each of them was attacking the other. I am thankful to be back at school.'

Night after night I would listen to the problems of youngsters and help them to sort themselves out. By the end of term I was completely exhausted and felt like a piece of chewed string.

I formed the practice of spending at least a week of each of the three vacations at a house of one of our Anglican religious communities. It was necessary not only to rest in peaceful surroundings, but also to endeavour to have the spiritual batteries recharged.

The community I went to least was Nashdom, the home of the English Benedictines. They inhabited a splendid mansion near Burnham, Buckinghamshire, which had been designed by Edwin Lutyens for Princess Alexis Dolgorouki. I never felt at home there, as their offices and worship were all in Latin and they were very Western in their outlook.

However, there was one very interesting link between Nashdom and Bryanston. There had been a puzzling number of thefts of valuable books from the school library. These were traced to a seller of secondhand books in Bournemouth, who informed us that they had been brought in for sale by one of the senior boys at Bryanston. We discovered that he had been in the clutches of a Black Magic group in the Bournemouth area; he had wanted the money partly to buy occult books and partly in order to go on orgiastic weekends in the holidays.

I had had no experience of Satanism but I knew that Nashdom's Father Robert Pettitpierre, OSB, had had considerable experience of Satanism and had helped to rescue many affected by this evil cult. When I mentioned this to our headmaster, he at once decided to visit Nashdom. The community, with its extreme Anglo-Catholic ways, was like nothing he had ever experienced before. However, he made friends with the abbot and it was arranged for the boy to spend several weeks at Nashdom. When he returned he was apparently cured of his addiction.

Later the abbot was invited to come to preach to the school. He was obviously ill-at-ease and unaccustomed to being with boys. Perhaps because of shyness, when he met a group of prefects he told them some rather risqué stories, perhaps in an attempt to break the ice. They were deeply shocked and his sermon to the school was not a success.

But there is little doubt that the Nashdom Community gave some excellent priests to the Church, notably Gregory Dix, the great liturgical scholar, and Dom Bernard who, when he was appointed vicar of All Saints, Margaret Street, brought a new warmth and spirit of friendliness to the then rather frigid and correct shrine of Anglo-Catholicism, as well as becoming one of the outstanding preachers in London.

Sometimes I stayed at Kelham, the mother house of the Society of the Sacred Mission.

This community, founded by the inimitable Father Kelly, had played an important part in the training of ordinands. During the years when there was no help available from State grants or Church bursaries, they provided training for boys from poor backgrounds who they felt had a vocation for the priesthood. As, frequently, they came from elementary schools, they had first to undertake a preliminary course to fill the gaps in their education. Then they began a fairly long theological course, the Kelham fathers providing the tutors and lecturers.

Members of the community and the young men in training all lived together in one large house. It seemed a spartan but somewhat boisterous life. There was a most impressive chapel, with a great rood screen and a Calvary carved by Jagger.

When I first stayed there, the director-general was Father Tribe, a wise and cultured priest who was, most sadly, killed later during an air raid on London.

Kelham gave the Church a number of faithful priests, but in 1971 the liberal establishment of bishops decided it should be closed, doubtless because they thought it gave too monastic an environment for ordinands.

More frequently I stayed at Cowley, in the mother house of the Cowley fathers. The Society of St John the Evangelist, a community of mission priests, was founded in 1865 by Father Benson (then vicar of Cowley, Oxford) and is thus the oldest

Anglican Community for men. At its height, SSJE did valuable missionary work in Cape Town, Pondoland, Poona, Bombay, the USA and elsewhere.

Sadly, in recent years there have been few vocations to the Order and they have had to contract their work. Their spacious home at Marston Street, Oxford, with its fine church, is now occupied by St Stephen's House, the theological college. SSJE still operate from St Edward's House, in the shadow of Westminster Abbey, where their ministry is of inestimable value to the Church in London and beyond. In recent years their Father Superior has been Father David Campbell, son of Admiral Campbell, who was given his VC for services with Q ships in the First World War.

Cowley fathers have always been much in demand for parish Missions and for Lent courses, and have been widely used as confessors and spiritual advisors. Their branch in the USA seems to have a number of younger recruits and it may well be that in the providence of God there will be a re-flowering and renewal of the community.

They have had some wonderful men in their order, such as Father Wagget, whose preaching drew packed churches in the early years of this century, and Father Callaway, who laboured for years in the Mission of St Cuthbert (in Pondoland) and wrote so attractively about it. Father Callaway's ministry in South Africa was in the heroic days of missionary work. He went on trek and covered long distances on horseback in the Drakensburg mountains, often camping out and living very simply with Africans in their kraals.

Years later I got to know Father Sedding, when he came out to St John's, Territet, for Holy Week services. He had formed the habit, for some time, of taking up, each year or two, a special subject for study in his recreation periods. At one time it might be flowers, at another trees or butterflies or stars. When he came out to the Canton Vaud his subject was rocks. I can remember him on his day off, with his Cowley cassock tucked up in his belt, scrambling like a chamois over the crags above Jaman, knocking off specimens of rock with his hammer. At the end of his stay I saw him off from Montreux station and had the greatest difficulty in lifting up his suitcase, as it was full of specimens of rock.

I found my first retreat at Cowley somewhat austere. The windows in my room were glazed over, presumably to prevent retreatants being distracted by the outside world. Meals in the refectory were sparse, to say the least, and served on chipped enamel plates. But nothing could detract from the joy and peace and sense of holiness. Cowley has always been loyal to the teaching of the Prayer Book as well as faithful to the beauty and discipline of Catholic spirituality. Like many other Anglicans, I shall always be grateful to the Cowley fathers for their help and example.

The community I knew best was the Community of the Resurrection, at Mirfield, West Yorkshire, founded by Bishop Charles Gore in 1892.

When I first went to Mirfield, one emerged from the railway station under a grim dark arch and walked through a depressing street of grey little mill-workers' houses. The main industry of the West Riding then was the wool textile trade. Giant woollen mills stood all around, each with its tall factory chimney belching out smoke. All the buildings were grimed with smoke; I remember that even the rose bushes in the community garden were so grimy with soot that they made the hands filthy. From their grounds could be seen, looking towards Huddersfield, about fifty factory chimneys. To the eyes of a Southerner, it was a most depressing environment and any young man coming with romantic ideas of the monastic life would have had a severe test of his vocation.

The home of the community had been a large and solid Victorian merchant's house, in big grounds. The fathers added on a retreat wing for visitors and a separate building for their theological college. They also built a splendid and spacious chapel, with a large space round the altar and a *baldachino*, all rather reminiscent of Eastern Orthodox worship and not at all Latin.

Mirfield has given some outstanding priests to the Church.

Probably the best known to our generation is Trevor Huddleston. After years of devoted work in the slums of Sophiatown, Johannesburg, he wrote *Naught for Your Comfort*. This book probably did more to alert the world to the evils of apartheid than anything else that has been written. After Father Huddleston was recalled from South Africa, he served the Church as the suffragan bishop of Stepney, then as a bishop in Tanzania and afterwards as archbishop of the splendidly-named Province of the Indian Ocean, which includes Mauritius, the Seychelles and Madagascar. But always, up to and including today, he has been a leader in the fight against injustice and racial prejudice in South Africa.

When I first went to Mirfield, the superior was Father Keble Talbot. The elder son of the revered Bishop Talbot of Winchester, he came from a family which for centuries had bred leaders in Church and State. Almost any office of preferment in our Church would have been open to him. But he felt, rather to his father's disappointment, that God was calling him to be a monk and, until the end of a long life, he was a faithful son of the community. He was the friend and confidante of some of the leading figures in Church and State. Sometimes he would return from a weekend away at one of England's great country houses and regale his brethren, at mealtimes in the refectory or at recreation, with accounts of the sayings and doings of Cabinet ministers and other notabilities. He had an enchanting sense of humour and was a superb raconteur. But those who were privileged to hear his address given in conducted retreats were soon aware of the depth and wisdom of his spiritual teaching.

Some of the older members of the community came from privileged and cultured backgrounds. I remember the charm and courtesy of Cyril Bickersteth, of Father Hallward and Father Seyzinger. As the community grew in numbers, some came from quite humble backgrounds. The Community of the Resurrection has always had an astonishing diversity and variety in its membership. There have been eminent scholars like Bishop Walter Frere, Lionel Thornton and, of course, the founder, Bishop Gore.

In the early days some took an active part in the beginnings of Christian Socialism and Father Paul Bull shared platforms with Keir Hardy. Others had quite different gifts, like Father Beaumont, who had a wide friendship amongst actors and actresses and who, when he was a curate, would sit down with a cigarette at his lips and play popular music on the piano for rowdy singsongs.

I remember with affection the tall gaunt figure of Father Ralph Bell who, for years, was a kind of estate steward. He came from the North Riding gentry. Clad in khaki shirt and shorts, and wearing a panama hat, he would be found most afternoons in the grounds, bullying the novices and any hapless visitors he could impress into undertaking gardening or manual work on the estate.

Some of the Mirfield fathers had special gifts as preachers, like two superiors in later years: Jonathan Graham, who I had known as an undergraduate at King's College, Cambridge, and who died at a regrettably early age, in 1965; also Hugh Bishop who, as a prisoner-of-war, had exercised a wonderful ministry in prisoner-of-war camps and who later developed a remarkable gift of giving arresting addresses to large audiences on TV. Unfortunately, he left the community in sad circumstances.

From its earliest days the community aimed to adapt the religious life to the changed circumstances of the modern age and to have, itself, a more democratic method of government. This year CR will be keeping the centenary of its foundation; in this period it has given to the Church at least ten bishops and a great number of scholars, teachers, missionaries, evangelists and confessors. Our whole Church will join in giving thanks for their life and witness.

The Society of St Francis was our near neighbour at Bryanston, their friary being at Hilfield, near Cerne Abbas. In 1931 the Bishop of Salisbury received the vows of Brother Douglas (who had been a master at Eton before he was ordained) and two lay brothers, making their Profession as the Brotherhood of St Francis of Assisi at Cerne Abbas.

About the same time, Father George Potter and a few brothers launched the Brotherhood of the Holy Cross, to care for homeless boys and serve the poor of Peckham (in south London).

Also during this period, Father Algy Robertson had become vicar of St Ives, in the county of Huntingdonshire. He had run his vicarage with an ever-open door, rather on Franciscan lines, as he had been greatly influenced by *Christa Seva Sangha*, an attempt to adapt the Franciscan life to Indian conditions.

It seemed right that these three groups, who had been trying to introduce the Franciscan life into the Church of England, should join forces. In 1937, Father Algy left St Ives to become novice master of the combined brotherhood at Cerne Abbas, Brother Douglas remaining the father minister.

For years Brother Douglas continued his work for homeless tramps, found as he walked the roads himself and sometimes slept in the workhouses, while maintaining a home for wayfarers at Cerne Abbas. Meanwhile, Father Algy slowly organised a religious community, training its novices, arranging its round of daily services and building the spiritual life of the Brotherhood. He combined this with incessant travel all over the country, fulfilling a busy programme of visits to universities and public schools, sermons and Missions in parishes, and countless appointments with individuals, to give counsel or hear confessions.

It was said that Father Algy left, all over the land, a trail of broken engagements, unanswered letters and devoted friends. He had no sense of punctuality, probably because he was so engrossed by the person he was talking to that he could not bear to part and so was late for the next appointment.

In appearance he was short and somewhat tubby, with a penetrating, almost squeaky, voice. He had a great love for people and a gift of understanding them and putting them at their ease. For years he had poor health, his digestive system probably having been undermined during the years he had spent in India, when he tried to live on the food of poor Indians rather than on that usually consumed by the *sahibs*. Sometimes he would have a hot-water bottle underneath his habit, held up by the girdle, and it is said that he deposited prescriptions for the medicine on which he depended at chemists' shops at all the main London termini.

Father Denis, SSF, recounted how Father Algy was a familiar figure on many fast mainline trains, as he travelled far and wide to keep his appointments: Father Denis recollected how the buffet stewards on one Southern Region express kept a minute's silence on the day of Father Algy's funeral, in memory of the little figure in the brown cloak and skull cap.

For much of this information I am indebted to the excellent biography by Father Denis, but I had the good fortune to meet and be with Father Algy on a number of occasions. He died (aged sixty-one) in 1955, worn out by his nights of prayer and letter-writing, his constant travelling and his incessant work in building up the Society of St Francis.

I did not know Brother Douglas, the co-founder, so well. He was often away from the friary, as his gifts seemed to lie in starting new ventures and blazing fresh trails. One of his most remarkable endeavours came at the end of the war, when he was one of the first to build bridges between the defeated (and often starving) Germans and ourselves. At Hamburg he ran, for a while, a club for wounded German soldiers, where those with legs and no arms found and dragged in wood, with which toys were made by men who had arms but no legs.

Today SSF have fifteen houses for their work in various parts of Great Britain. In addition, there are five houses for women members of the Community of St Francis, as well as a Convent of Poor Clares who, from their enclosure and hidden life of prayer, uphold the active works of their Franciscan brothers and sisters. Brother Douglas was the founder and Father Algy was, to a large extent, the builder, but God has given the increase – and the growth in one generation is truly amazing.

We were most fortunate, at Bryanston, to have the Franciscans as our neighbours and I am glad there was regular contact between us.

In her great book *Worship*, Evelyn Underhill* put into better

* Underhill, Evelyn, *Worship*, London, Nisbet, 1936. Evelyn Underhill was an eminent Anglican writer on the spiritual life.

words than I can ever find, the value and importance of the religious orders in the Church of England. She wrote:

> But the greatest expression of this spirit of adoration, and perhaps the greatest achievement of the Anglican revival when seen in spiritual regard – is the restoration of Religious Orders within the English Church. For the Religious Life sums up and expresses in a living symbolism, the ideal consummation of all worship; the total oblation of the creature to the purposes of God. No church within which these sacrificial dispositions are not produced, and which does not possess the hidden power-houses of surrendered personalities, the consecrated channels of its adoring and redeeming love, has risen to the full possibilities of the Christian call; or proclaimed in the only language which carries conviction, the unlimited demand of God upon the soul.

I can only say that in my life, again and again, I have found refreshment and inspiration, renewed hope and fresh vision, through the help I have been given by members of our religious orders.

From the start of my work at Bryanston, I realised clearly that I did not carry the guns of my predecessor as chaplain.

The Reverend J C Winslow received his education at Eton, Balliol and Wells Theological College. He was a scholar, a classicist, a poet and hymn writer of no mean order. He went out to work in India before the First World War and soon found a great love for the Indian people, with a sympathetic insight into their political ambitions. With that went a deep longing to show them Our Lord as Saviour and to present the Gospel without the accretions imposed by the British Raj.

He had been greatly impressed by some Hindu saints and mystics and wished to establish a Christian *ashram*, where the Indians and English could live together, sharing a simple life of prayer and study, linked with good works and humble service. In 1922 Father Winslow founded *Christa Seva Sangha* (the Society of Servants belonging to Christ). They wore cassocks of white homespun cloth, with a saffron girdle, and ate only the simplest of vegetarian food, the necessities of life being provided from a common fund. Father Winslow became *acharya* (superior) and the *ashram* slowly increased in disciples.

But (in 1933) Jack Winslow visited England on furlough and came under the influence of the Buchmanites (or the Oxford Movement), later to be known as Moral Rearmament. At that time the movement was having quite a vogue, especially at the universities and among affluent people: it was sometimes called 'The Salvation Army of the Upper Classes'. At a house party, Father Winslow came to the conviction that he could no longer remain *acharya* of the *Sangha*. This caused many sad hearts, some of the brethren remaining with the *ashram* although their founder had left them.

For a while Jack Winslow worked with the Buchmanite movement, but, after some time, he left them – although, to some extent, his subsequent work was always influenced by the pastoral method of the Oxford groups.

It was after this period that Mr Coade invited Winslow to come to Bryanston as chaplain. He was much liked and did good work but, shortly before I was appointed, the headmaster and housemasters had come to the conclusion that the somewhat intense methods of the Oxford groups did not make for a very healthy atmosphere amongst adolescent schoolboys. By mutual consent he resigned and became chaplain of Lee Abbey, the resident evangelical centre in North Devon.

One tradition which Jack Winslow established at Bryanston, and which I was very glad to continue, was the practice of taking boys away for a weekend retreat immediately before their confirmation. It was not easy to obtain the staff's consent in the middle of a busy term, but we used to take the confirmands away after lunch on a Saturday and remain in retreat until breakfast on the Monday; the confirmation service was held on the Monday afternoon. We went to the Retreat House at Glastonbury Abbey, which provided a peaceful and beautiful setting.

One of the things which has given me great happiness in my

ministry is the fact that, in the years at Bryanston, I introduced between four and five hundred youngsters to the practice of going into retreat. Usually I had a Franciscan to give the addresses and help me and many of the retreatants found the joy and blessing of making their confessions and receiving absolution.

One of the rewards of being a school chaplain was that, three times a year, we shared in the school holidays. In addition to the visits to monastic houses mentioned above, it was my practice each Holy Week to help in some parish or other, by giving addresses and assisting in the Easter services. One year I was invited to give the Holy Week addresses in the friary at Cerne Abbas. In other years I placed myself at the disposal of the father guardian, who had, each Lent, far more requests from parishes for preachers to give Holy Week addresses than he had men available.

I was a poor substitute for a friar, but I was able to help several hard-pressed parish priests, mainly in slum parishes in the north. Especially I remember a week at Rochdale (the home of Gracie Fields), where I met, amongst other parishioners, England's official hangman. As I shook hands with him, I could not help thinking how those hands had prepared the rope which had sent many men to their deaths.

Other visits which have stayed in my memory were to a dockland parish in Newcastle, and to one of the biggest working-class housing estates in England. This was at Braunstone, Leicester. About 30,000 people were living there, in innumerable streets of little semi-detached houses, which looked identical, and with scarcely a shop or club or pub in the parish. The vicar had an almost impossible task in trying to minister single-handed to the spiritual and social needs of such a vast parish.

Some of my holidays were occupied by visits to members of my family, who had been sadly neglected for much of the year, but most years during my time at Bryanston I organised a trip abroad and took a party of boys for what was often their first holiday on the Continent.

On several occasions, accompanied by another member of staff, I took a winter sports party to Switzerland. Amongst resorts we visited were Saanenmoser (near Gstaad), Adelboden and Zermatt. The advantage of going to Saanenmoser was that we found cheap accommodation in a friendly little hotel, yet could enjoy nearly all the ski runs of fashionable (and vastly expensive) Gstaad, which was a few miles away.

In the early years we took parties of a dozen or so but as, nearly always, one or other of the party broke a leg skiing, this became rather a hassle. So in later years I went with two or three older boys who had had some experience of skiing. We used to rent a chalet and do our own shopping and cooking, which cut down the expenses considerably. My earlier contacts with a family of guides at Zermatt helped in obtaining the chalet at reasonable cost.

Some years I took a group of Bryanston boys to the Alps in the summer, for a mountain-walking and climbing holiday. Amongst other mountain centres visited were Saas Fee, Zermatt, Zinal and Arolla.

In 1951 I took a party of six senior boys to Zermatt, accompanied by David Goodfield, then a young master. He later married the younger daughter of Mr and Mrs Coade and became headmaster of Churcher's College, Petersfield. To the grief of all his friends and family, he died quite young, after playing tennis.

We did quite a lot of hard mountain-walking and some of us had some instruction in rock-climbing on the Riffelhorn. We engaged Emil Perren, a well-known Zermatt guide who I had met before. Three of the party, as well as myself, were keen on attempting some bigger climbs, so for this expedition Emil brought along a fellow guide, Leo Kronig.

We went up the long path to the Rothorn mountain hut; it took four hours and at times we wondered if we would ever get off the long moraine path. Next morning the weather was bad. We climbed the Wellenkuppe, an easy climb, in thick mist. The

Climbing at Zermatt: (*from left*) Emil Perren, the Zermatt guide, K E J and Dick Harthan, a Bryanston housemaster

visibility at the top was nil and we found the climbing cold and unpleasant, but the rocks, though covered with snow, were fairly easy. When we got back to the hut we decided to stay there another night, hoping the weather would improve. We spent the day playing cards and sleeping, as it was snowing most of the time.

Next day was glorious, a perfect morning, so we set out early to climb the Zinal Rothorn. Emil Perren took John Cotton and me on one rope; Leo took the two other boys on another rope. There was a great deal of snow and the holds were all covered with snow or ice. Emil said afterwards that he had rarely, if ever, climbed the Zinal Rothorn under such bad conditions. We had a long hard fight with rocks, snow and a strong wind. It was the most difficult climbing I had ever done. From the top we had a glorious view of all the Alpine giants, especially the Matterhorn, but it was too cold to stay long. Emil hurried down the mountain at breakneck speed, in a foul temper.

We arrived back at the hut at 2 pm, only to find that one of the boys had badly frost-bitten fingers, which had turned yellow. He had torn one of his gloves on the crags, trying to grip icy ledges. He was also mountain-sick. After Emil had rubbed his fingers with snow, and massaged them, we walked slowly down the mountain and reached Zermatt at 6.45 pm. At once I took the boy, John Harper, to the village doctor, a splendid old Swiss. He said to John, 'What do you intend to do when you have left school?'

'I hope to qualify as a doctor – a surgeon.'

The old man replied, 'My son, there are many mountains but you only have one pair of hands. You must not attempt any more climbing this holiday.'

Meanwhile, John Cotton and I had set our hearts on having a go at the Matterhorn and Emil had thought that we were now ready to attempt it. However, I felt that it was too big a responsibility to permit the boy to make this climb without parental approval. Later that morning Mr Cotton had a tele-phone call in his Leicester office and heard John, in a weak voice, saying, 'Father, I am telephoning from the post office in Zermatt. Please may I climb the Matterhorn?'

The father thought for a moment and then said, 'Well, if you want to do it, I suppose you had better try it. But I will not tell your mother until you are down and off the mountain.'

For this kind of climb, a guide would take only one person on the rope. So it was arranged that Emil would be my guide and Leo Kronig would climb with John Cotton. Later that day we left on the five-hour walk up to the Belvedere hut.

We were up at 4 am next morning and started our climb at 5 am. It was a perfect morning but there was a lot of snow on the Matterhorn and conditions underfoot were not good. In good conditions, when the rocks are dry and warm, the mountain is not considered a difficult climb by modern standards. There are fixed ropes to help climbers at some of the difficult pitches, but we found that the fixed ropes were glazed with ice and frozen stiff. I found it fairly comfortable going up to the Solvay hut, a small rescue hut which is about halfway up. But above that it was very tricky work. We reached the summit at 10 am, having found that the final slope was a real toil up in deep snow. We only spent fifteen minutes on the summit as, although the view was indescribably beautiful and breathtaking, we were frozen with cold.

I found that coming down was more scaring and difficult than the ascent. We were feeling very exhausted and the long descent down the mountain seemed interminable. Eventually we reached the Belvedere hut at 3 pm. I felt so dehydrated that I drank fourteen cups of tea. After a long rest, we walked slowly home and reached Zermatt village at 7 pm. Later that night, after dinner, John and I, with our two guides, drank a bottle of Swiss wine in celebration.

In later years, after he had come down from King's College, Cambridge, John Cotton offered himself for ordination and was trained at Cuddesdon. He was a devoted young priest but, unfortunately, he began his ministry at a period of much doubt and uncertainty. It was the era of books like *Honest to God*, by Bishop Robinson, and many people had become somewhat disorientated. For a time John felt that it was right for him not to continue as a full-time priest so, for a while, he worked as a personal therapist in a big mental hospital. Shortly afterwards he went into hospital for what seemed like a routine operation for the removal of his appendix, but died suddenly from per-itonitis.

His death came as a grievous shock to me and I believe it was a great loss to the Church, for I am confident he would have come through his 'dark night of the soul' and would have developed into a wise and greatly loved priest.

In my last year at Bryanston, I was asked to go out and conduct Holy Week services at the English church at Monte Carlo.

No doubt many people would think of Monte Carlo more in

connection with its casino than with Church activities but the Anglican church in Monaco was very active and well supported. Probably there are as many lonely, sad and sick folk there as in many places. It was well that I was there, as the English chaplain at Menton had been taken ill, so I was there on Easter Day ministering to quite large congregations.

When my duties were over, I met the newly appointed head-master of Bryanston, Robson Fisher, who flew out to Nice to meet me. We hired a little Fiat and had a delightful week touring in Provence.

But my time at Bryanston was drawing to an end. Never in my ministry had I sought preferment or promotion. I had been taught that it was right to stay where you were until asked, or told, to go somewhere else. But I knew that, in my work of teaching, I was becoming very stale, so I had decided that it would be right to accept the first reasonable offer I was made to work anywhere else.

There was a vacancy at Beaulieu, in the New Forest. One of the members of the PCC, a naval officer, suggested to the patron that the living should be offered to his old naval chaplain: the Reverend John Wallis. Wallis was one of my near neighbours but, as he had only recently been appointed to his parish, he felt he could not leave it and suggested that they should ask me. So, eventually, I was asked to become vicar of Beaulieu.

I had known and loved the village and the abbey church for years, so I was delighted. It became my first, and only, incumbency. As I was then aged fifty-four, and had been ordained for twenty-seven years without ever having had a living of my own, I did not feel I had been unduly careerist.

It was a hard wrench to leave Bryanston. I had become involved not only with the boys, but with the staff, their wives and their children. I had taken as much interest as I could in the small local village and had, for years, run a Children's Service in the parish church for the children of staff and villagers. I had been very happy indeed in my twelve years at the school and had made some lifelong friends.

So I left Bryanston with a heavy heart, but tremendously

grateful for all that the school community had given me. Though, after twelve years in the specialist ministry of a school chaplain, it was delightful to return to the ordered round of parochial life.

4
Portsmouth and Stansted
1940–1948

Heaven's light our guide
The motto of the city of Portsmouth

I arrived in Portsmouth in May 1940, to take up my appointment on the staff of St Mary's, Portsea, as priest-in-charge of the mission church of St Wilfrid. St Mary's was, perhaps, one of the best known parishes in the Church of England. Two of its vicars had later become archbishops (Cosmo Gordon Lang and Cyril Garbett) and a number of its curates ended their lives as bishops.

The builder of the modern parish was Edgar Jacob, later bishop of St Albans. He became vicar in 1878 and by 1892 was convinced that it was necessary to pull down the parish church and build a much bigger one. A larger church was, indeed, needed. In 1881 the population of the parish was 24,000. By the end of the century, owing to the vast increase in the number of personnel at the naval dockyard, the population had grown to 47,000.

J G Lockhart,[*] in his biography of Cosmo Gordon Lang, describes the parochial terrain:

> It was the mother parish of the greater part of Portsmouth, excluding the old town but including a wilderness of sprawling suburbs. The people were mostly naval men and their families, dockyard workers and artisans.

Instead of splitting up this vast parish into several smaller parishes, the policy of Canon Jacob was to have an imposing parish church surrounded by several mission churches, served by a

* Lockhart, J G, *Cosmo Gordon Lang*, London, Hodder and Stoughton Ltd, 1949.

large staff working from a common centre, the Clergy House. At its peak, the number of curates reached sixteen.

The new church was built at a cost of £44,000 (which represents around £1 million in today's money). £28,000 of this came in gifts, at first anonymous, from the then First Lord of the Admiralty, the Right Honourable W H Smith. No doubt he felt some responsibility for the immense growth of the parish following the expansion of the naval dockyard.

Canon Jacob also built five mission churches, each about ten or fifteen minutes' walk from the parish church. During the incumbency of Cosmo Gordon Lang, Evensong was at 6.30 pm and when the great church (which could seat over a thousand) was full, the overflow would go on to one of the mission churches, where the service was timed to begin fifteen minutes later.

When I first arrived at the Clergy House, in Fratton Road, my first feeling was of acute depression at the drabness of the miles of little mean streets which surrounded it. Having just come from Territet, looking across Lake Leman to the mountains of Savoy, the ugliness of Portsmouth hit me between the eyes. The city was extremely congested, most of the little terraced houses being built right on to the pavement, without any front gardens.

St Wilfrid's was in the 'West End' of the parish. It was not in any sense a slum area. Most of the houses were occupied by naval petty officers and ratings, or by foremen and shop stewards from the dockyard. It was St Faith's Mission, in Landport, which was involved in really rough slum conditions.

St Wilfrid's was built in 1908, when Cyril Garbett, then a curate, was priest-in-charge. Garbett planned and designed it himself. He was much in advance of the ideas of his time, for he designed what the Americans would call an 'excellent plant'. The church was light and spacious (seating 250) and under the same big roof was a large concert hall with a platform, big club-rooms, kitchens and toilets. In later years a dignified high altar was built, flanked by imposing Corinthian pillars and covered by a *baldachino*.

Cyril Garbett was vicar of the parish from 1909 to 1919. He was a strict disciplinarian, if not a martinet; woe betide the unfortunate curate who was found in his room after 2.30 pm and not out visiting.

Until 1914 cassocks were not worn out in the streets, but the clergy were garbed in what was the customary dress of a clergyman: a silk hat and frock coat. Their evenings were very full, with attendances at boys' clubs, Scout and Guide parades, men's meetings, preparation classes for Sunday School teachers and confirmation classes. In 1912 there were nearly 4,000 names on the Sunday School registers (in 1988 this had dropped to 88). The annual summer outings for Sunday School children must have been a great feat in organisation and crowd management: in 1891, 1,600 children went on a day's outing to Leigh Park.

Garbett had a tremendous capacity for hard work and, during his years at Portsea, laid the foundation for the national leadership which he later exercised at Winchester and York.

But to me the great hero of St Mary's, Portsea, was not Lang or Garbett, but Canon Lovell Southam, who succeeded Garbett in 1919. He inherited a tremendous, if not crushing, weight of tradition. But he was a man of great courage and strong convictions and gradually he brought in needed changes in patterns of worship and parochial work.

He introduced a Sung Communion service at 9.30 am and began using vestments (at first simple linen ones). A light breakfast was held in the institute after the service, to enable those who had abstained from food beforehand to break their fast together.

The importance of prayer was a vital part of his teaching. He encouraged the keener people to go into retreat each year and he was largely responsible for the opening of the diocesan retreat house at Catherington. There was considerable opposition among some members of the congregation to the changes. Until 1919 the candles on the altar had never been lit and there seemed a lot of Protestant prejudice lingering in the city. But Southam continued in his teaching with courage and persistence.

When he resigned through ill-health in 1927, his diocesan bishop wrote, at the time of the appointment of Southam's successor, Geoffrey Lunt: 'When Lovell Southam resigned from St Mary's, the parish was at the nadir of its history as to finance, staff and effective prestige.'

But, a year later, Geoffrey Lunt reported to his bishop that he found amongst a section of his communicants:

... a more highly developed spiritual and devotional life than is to be found, I believe, in the majority of parishes. Through intensive teaching and through regular use of Catherington Retreat House there has grown up in the parish a small body of splendidly trained people; and without this nucleus I should view our future with sheer dismay.

When I arrived in Portsea, the vicar was Canon Robins, who later (in 1943) was appointed dean of Salisbury cathedral. He was a kind and wise vicar. His son, John, joined the RAF and was sent to Singapore. He was made a prisoner-of-war by the Japanese and for over a year his parents had no news of him. With the anxiety which this caused him, and with the strain of war conditions, the health of Canon Robins suffered badly and he became ill with anaemia. But he recovered sufficiently to be installed into the deanery of Salisbury.

By 1940 the staff of curates was reduced to seven. The Clergy House had been partly commandeered as the HQ for the RAF officers in command of the balloon barrage which protected Portsmouth. For a year or so we had a combined Mess of seven curates and six RAF officers. There was probably no other Mess like it anywhere, but it worked happily and prevented my colleagues and me from talking ecclesiastical shop at mealtimes.

I found that St Wilfrid's had long had a tradition of a weekly parish Communion with parish breakfast. So convinced were they of the value of the breakfast that this was continued all through the war years, the people bringing their own rations as the rationing authorities would make no allowances for such gatherings. At one period of severe air-raids, the Sunday Eucharist was celebrated at five separate altars on five consecutive Sundays, one being the headmaster's desk at the nearby primary school, when an unexploded bomb was sitting outside our church vestry. But there was no halt in the Sunday worship and always some of the faithful came.

Daylight raids by Nazi planes on Portsmouth began in June 1940. One of my memories of that summer of 1940 was of a small camp for boys which I ran in August. I collected half-a-dozen boys who had not been evacuated from the city and we went for a lightweight camp in the grounds of the house of one of my friends at Beaulieu, in the New Forest. We left Portsmouth by bus, having to change at Southampton into another bus to take us on to Brockenhurst. When we reached Southampton, the air-raid sirens went and I had to take the boys down into an air-raid shelter in the main square at Southampton. It was quite a heavy raid on Southampton docks, in which a great deal of damage was done. After the all-clear siren had sounded, we resumed our journey, our bus having to pick its way slowly through debris and shattered glass on the road to Brockenhurst.

It was against the Defence Regulations to erect tents near the coast. So, for a week, we slept in a woodshed in my friend's garden. On several occasions there were raids on Southampton, six miles away. We watched one daylight raid when German planes leisurely picked out and shot down, one by one, the sausage balloons that formed the balloon barrage for Southampton docks.

On another occasion, while we were cooking our midday stew on our wood fire, a stray German plane flew in from the Channel and came quite low. We dived into a nearby ditch, leaving our stew in the dixie to look after itself until things quietened down.

At night the anti-aircraft guns, which were hidden in the forest near our camp, would open up a fierce salvo and shrapnel would fall on the branches and leaves of nearby trees; on one occasion there was a patter of small lumps of shrapnel on the corrugated iron roof on our shed. As we lay in our sleeping-bags, I wondered whether it was right to have boys away in camp under such conditions, but then I reflected that they were much safer in the woods round Beaulieu than they would have been in their homes near Portsmouth naval dockyard.

We had a very happy week at our little camp and returned to Portsmouth much cheered and refreshed.

By mid-October there had been 226 day and night air-raid warnings. I had been assigned as a helper at a homeless centre at George Street School.

After the first bad raid I arrived there to find that about 120 bombed-out and rather shell-shocked people had arrived. In those early days of bombing the arrangements for bombed-out people were in a very primitive stage. The schoolchildren had been evacuated and there was a stock of mattresses and blankets in the empty classrooms. We had to bed the people down on the ground, the men in one room and the women in another.

The centres were staffed by volunteer helpers, mainly middle-aged and elderly women, largely recruited from the local churches. I used to admire the way some of these old folk would turn out, wearing tin hats and carrying their gas-masks, sometimes walking through the dark streets before the raid was over in order to open up the centre.

After a few days the people in the homeless centres would be taken out by bus to new homes in the country. But in the early months they had to remain in their cheerless quarters of the school for a week or two.

I have vivid memories of Christmas Day, 1940. There had been a severe raid on Portsmouth two nights before and our centre was full of bombed-out people. They had arrived in dazed groups, each one bringing a few belongings salvaged from the ruin of their homes and some pathetically clutching, in wrapped parcels, the gifts they had intended for Christmas presents. The lunch on Christmas Day was cold spam and boiled potatoes, washed down with tea. That afternoon I toured round all the public houses in the neighbourhood, appealing to the patrons to bring in gifts of Christmas fare. The response was overwhelming and heart-warming. That evening we had a splendid feast: cold turkey, Christmas puddings and mince pies, trifles, jellies and fruit salad, plus sweets and toys for the children. After the feast we had games for the children and a splendid singsong. It was wonderful how, for an hour or so, people put aside their fears and worries and, perhaps for the sake of the children, gave themselves up to cele- brating Christmas.

As the water level in Portsea Island was very near the surface, the people could not have underground shelters. Instead, brick shelters were built in the streets. These would have given no shelter at all in the case of a direct hit but may have given some protection against shrapnel or blasting. During the winter of 1940–1941, night after night the shelters would be filled as the air-raid warning sirens sounded. There the people would remain, sometimes for hours, in the cold; each shelter containing about a hundred people sitting on benches in long lines facing each other. From St Wilfrid's we would go out to visit the twelve or so shelters in our district. Sometimes, helped by our senior Scouts, we would bring a dixie of cocoa. Soon we organised, in most shelters, short singsongs on the lines I had learned in the City of London the previous winter. On Sundays we carried round hymn books and had a short service.

Some of the raids in our area were most unpleasant. On several occasions I found myself crawling about the ruins of a recently demolished house searching for survivors. In the early days of the war the rescue services were not very organised and neighbours had to do what they could until demolition squads and ambulances arrived. More than once I had to scrabble in the debris with my bare hands until I felt the warm flesh of someone's face and gouged the choking dust out of throat and eyes and ears until, gradually, the whole body could be released and extricated.

Once, in a narrow alley during a raid, I came across a body

lying on the ground in a pool of blood. The man had had the top of his head blown off by shrapnel. I had done a little First Aid, through instructing small Boy Scouts to pass their tests, but I had never seriously thought I would be applying the bandages myself in real life. However, by the light of my torch, I slapped a large lump of cotton-wool over his head and kept it in place with a large triangular bandage. Next day I visited the casualty department at our local hospital to see if he was still alive and was surprised and cheered to see him sitting up in bed and smoking a cigarette.

On 10 January 1941, Portsmouth had its great fire blitz. That evening we were holding a parish party at St Wilfrid's. Soon after the sirens went, flares began dropping and we knew we were in for a big raid. Many hundreds of small incendiary bombs were dropped all round our mission. Many of the houses were empty, as the people used to go out of the city at sundown and camp out in the suburbs above Portsdown Hill, to escape the bombing.

These little incendiary bombs would crash through the roofs of the houses and lodge between ceiling and floor of the ground rooms, fizzing away like giant fireworks. We found that the best technique to deal with them was to use a spade to break the front windows of the empty houses and then thrust the spade up into the ceiling, scoop out the blazing bomb and throw it out through a window. The boys of my youth club, who had come for the party, much enjoyed this exercise. Later, they were extremely useful, climbing on to our church roof and helping to put out fires which had started on the roof.

By midnight the whole city of Portsmouth seemed on fire: it was possible to read a newspaper in the streets by the light of the flames.

The first raid started at 7 pm and continued until 9 pm. According to the interesting record of the blitz published by the *Portsmouth Evening News*, 25,000 incendiary bombs were dropped on the city in a few hours, as well as a number of devastating high explosive bombs.

There was a lull of two hours, while the dazed citizens came out of their shelters and tried to deal with the fires which were blazing everywhere. At 11.30 pm a second wave of bombers came in, lobbing their bombs down into the blazing inferno. This time the raid lasted for two hours.

Early in the raid the main 12-inch water-main had been ruptured, so there was no pressure and scarcely any water in the fire hydrants. There was no lack of fire engines and firemen, as the authorities had known earlier in the evening that Portsmouth was the target for the night, having learned to interpret the beam sent out by the Luftwaffe to guide their pilots to their destination. Fire appliances had been coming into the city all the evening from towns and cities all over the south of England but, without water, there was little that the firemen could do. They had the additional problem that, with fire appliances coming from various cities and counties, the nozzles of their hose-pipes would not always fit together, so they could not make a long line to pump water from the sea.

The glow of the burning city could be seen from many miles away, even from as far as the coast of France. The tall tower of the Guildhall stood out like a blazing torch. This great building, one of the finest town halls in the country, became a smoking shell, the interior completely eaten by fire. It was six days before the building was cool enough for salvage parties to enter.

Three main shopping centres, at Kings Road and Palmerston Road, Southsea, and Commercial Road, Portsmouth, were completely destroyed and reduced to rubble. Amongst other buildings destroyed were six churches, including the Roman Catholic cathedral, three cinemas, a hospital and a theatre. Huge areas of the narrow streets and small dwellings were bombed into ruins. During this raid 171 people were killed, many hundreds seriously injured and an estimated 3,000 made homeless.

By what seemed a miracle, the great parish church was not seriously damaged, although the St Barnabas Mission was demolished and St Faith's and St Wilfrid's badly damaged. But St Mary's stood up amongst the surrounding rubble and ruins, rather as St Paul's Cathedral stood out against the surrounding devastation in the City of London.

A few days after the raid, the vicar's secretary jotted down these lines in her notebook:

Many telephones still working. Bread by lorry from Reading.
No electricity; no water in parts; gas at low pressure
13th. Some electricity back
14th. Communal kitchen opened at St Faith's
20th. Water in again; electricity at Vicarage

The raids on Portsmouth continued until the early summer, but gradually eased in their ferocity and by August they had almost ceased, apart from the occasional hit-and-run raid.

There were severe raids in March when, for the first time, great mines were dropped by parachute and caused immense damage. On this occasion, on a bright moonlit night, I saw a parachute slowly coming down in the large grounds of Kingston cemetery. I was not very far away and, thinking that perhaps the parachute was conveying an airman who had baled out from his plane, I ran towards it. Fortunately I did not get very close, for the parachute mine exploded on impact with the ground and big lumps of tombstone began hurtling all round me.

There was another very severe raid in April. By then, nineteen of Portsmouth's churches had been put out of action. Altogether, during the war, Portsmouth had 50 air-raids, during which 930 people were killed and 1,300 were seriously wounded. About 7,000 homes were destroyed.

Incidentally, the then provost of Portsmouth cathedral scored a very black mark in my book, as it was his practice to leave the city before nightfall, to escape the bombing, leaving his people in the cathedral parish to face the music.

Through all these wartime months and years, the parochial life and work continued as normally as possible. There were a great number of funerals, especially after bad bombing, and once, following a succession of severe raids, I had to commit to the ground bodies in boxes, as the supply of coffins had run out.

When a cruiser or destroyer put in for repairs in the dockyard, there was a sudden rush of weddings hastily arranged. On one occasion I had the pleasant task of conducting a mass wedding for five couples; the bridegrooms were all sailors, who, according to naval custom, wore large white silk bows with their blue jacket uniform. I had to be especially alert, to make sure I was joining together the right couples from the row lined up before me.

At some periods of the war, for months at a time I did not go outside the city. When the pressure eased a bit, it was wonderful to have a day off, out in the countryside and away from the shattered houses and war-scarred streets.

I remember especially one such day when, in glorious spring sunshine, I took a train journey to nearby Chichester. While having a drink in one of the inns, I heard Churchill's voice on the radio. He was making one of his greatest war speeches, one of those that brought such hope and comfort to a hard-pressed people at a very difficult time.

In the afternoon I slipped into the coolness and peace of the cathedral. I shall always remember a young RAF sergeant who came into the great church. Kneeling down in a side chapel, he took a rosary from his pocket and remained still and erect for fifteen minutes while he was telling his beads. I had always thought of the rosary as a specifically Roman devotion and a form of prayer not usually adopted by Anglicans, but I could not help wondering to myself how many young Anglicans would know what to say or think if they were asked to remain kneeling for fifteen minutes in silent prayer.

That same afternoon, in a church shop, I bought myself a rosary and for many years I have found it the greatest help in my devotional life. It is strange to me that so few Anglican priests seem to teach their people to use it. After all, thirteen of the fifteen Mysteries of the rosary are incidents in the life of Our Lord, as recorded in the New Testament. Only two refer to nonscriptural events: the Assumption of the Blessed Virgin is not taught as part of the doctrine of our Church, but many Anglicans have for long meditated on the 'Falling Asleep of the Mother of Christ' and it is exceedingly good for us to think sometimes not only of Mary's death but of the end of our own lives. Some Anglicans, again, would not find it easy to meditate on the 'Coronation of the Virgin', but could well be helped by recollecting the words from the Book of Revelation: 'Be thou faithful unto death and I will give thee a crown of life.'

A wider use of the rosary by Church of England clergy and laity would assuredly lead to a deepening understanding of mental prayer.

Each summer of the war I took youngsters from Portsmouth away to camp. I had become assistant district commissioner of the Portsmouth Scout Association and used to run combined camps for troops who were without a scoutmaster. Our favourite campsite was at Rogate, West Sussex, where my own troop camped often at weekends – and for a longer time in August.

As Defence Regulations prohibited tents anywhere near the coast, we used to pitch our tents in the woods above Rogate Lodge and camouflage them, by throwing over the ridge-poles nets interleaved with bracken and ferns. Boys of that era seemed to be a tougher breed than some of the rather spoiled generation of today. My youngsters used to pile their gear into their trek-cart, take this to pieces at Fratton station and load it into the guard's van, then disembark at Petersfield station and haul it the six miles to our campsite.

The kind owners of Rogate Lodge were the Misses Wyndham, sisters of the Lord Lieutenant of Sussex, Lord Leconfield of Petworth House. I have pleasant memories of these two somewhat prim and elderly spinsters kneeling down on the ground in our chapel tent for a Sunday Eucharist, surrounded by a crowd of somewhat scruffy-looking little urchins clad in shirts and shorts.

On one occasion, while we were all asleep in our tents at our camp hide-out, an armoured brigade of Canadian artillery moved in quietly during the night. When we woke up, we found that we were camping in the middle of an army brigade.

As we got nearer to D-Day in 1944, Portsmouth became an even more exciting place in which to live. All the roads leading to the south coast were lined by miles of parked tanks, personnel carriers, guns and lorries, all carefully camouflaged. Every creek and river and inlet along the coast was full of landing-craft and invasion barges.

A few days before the invasion, I managed to bluff my way across to Ryde, by using an out-of-date pass which I had saved from previous hospital visits. The Solent was an incredible sight. One could almost have walked across the four miles from Portsmouth to Ryde, so close was the press of the waiting destroyers and gunboats, landing-craft, barges and transports. A huge floating platform, about the size of two or three football pitches, was anchored in the middle of Spithead, to be used for loading and transferring supplies. The assembled flotilla stretched as far as the eye could see and was an amazing demonstration of the power and scope of Allied planning.

When, on the morning of D-Day, we heard on the radio that the invasion of Europe had begun, I went up to the top of the church tower, as no civilians were allowed near the front.

Looking over the roofs of the city to Spithead and the Solent, I could see the great armada on the move, carrying our men to the beaches of Normandy. It was an awe-inspiring sight.

By the end of 1944 I had become completely exhausted, in mind and body and soul, after the battering we had had for over four years. One glorious autumn day I had a long walk on my own along the South Downs near Butser Hill and Harting. I needed to think. Just before this, I had read an article in the *British Weekly* (the Nonconformist journal) which had greatly impressed me. It was written by their columnist 'Watchman':

... every man has his liberated moments, has even his great hours; it is only good sense and it may even be a sense of appreciation and gratitude to Him with whom in our solitudes we all have to do, to *arise* at the summons of such opportunities to break new ground. There is a passage in the Gospels which concludes (as it seems to me) some urgent lesson which Our Lord has been giving, probably to his chosen group of disciples. For the incident is closed in the text by a very abrupt set of words. We read 'These things spake Jesus and departed and did hide himself from them.' What were the very things which Jesus said there and then, after which He abruptly left them?

. . . 'Walk in the light lest darkness come upon you.' And later but still in the same breath 'While ye have light, believe in the light.' Was it that He was announcing to these simple men who had attached themselves to Him that life was like that? You are proceeding on your usual way when something, as we say, occurs to us. We should do well to 'stop and look and listen'. For such instants are not casual or superficial. They are on the contrary, the incidents furthest removed in their source and origin, more deeply beneath the surface of our life, than any other incidents which we can account for and later explain . . . A leap in the dark is never really asked of any of us. And what is that leap in the light but the leap upon the line of deeper evidences, the stirrings, the misgivings with their rebukes and corrections, of which we are capable and which we have experienced, and which make this final leap almost a necessity of thought.

In the same issue of the *British Weekly* there was a sermon from the Reverend Jas Reid, DD, on the response God asks, and from it I wrote down these words:

The love of God will ask a great deal. It will claim our interest in others, perhaps in people we never thought we could be interested in. It will claim us for purposes and plans that lie very far outside our own lives. 'He leadeth them out' was Christ's description of the Good Shepherd. What we sometimes need to see and to see till it becomes a vital truth, is that the way of salvation is the way of release from ourselves into the needs and service of others. When we are asked to take some live interest in a piece of work for the Kingdom we must not turn it down; it is the highest privilege.

These words seemed to speak to my condition. A few days later I went to see my vicar and told him that, with the greatest regret, I had decided to resign my curacy, and was asking the Community of the Resurrection if I could stay with them for a while at Mirfield, to try my vocation for the religious life.

When I had first come to the parish I had been made miserably sad at the ugliness of the inner city. But, when the train bore me out from Fratton station, I wept as I thought of the happiness I had found in the previous five years and the friends I was leaving behind. The little terraced houses were monotonously the same, but the people who lived in them were gloriously different – and they had been magnificent.

After the strain of the five war years, it was wonderful to have time for reading and quiet prayer at Mirfield. Amongst other books, I found especially helpful Dom Cuthbert Butler's great book, *Ways of Christian Life*, with its exposition of Benedictine spirituality – and the later teaching of Cistercians, Franciscans, Dominicans and many others. The books that influenced me most were: *Holy Wisdom* – Father Augustine Baker; *The Mystical Element of Religion* – Baron Friedrich von Hugel; *Life of St Teresa* and her *Interior Castle* – E A Peers; *Riddle of the N T* – E C Hoskyns and F N Davey; *The Gospel and Human Needs* – Father F N Figgis; *Vision of God* – Bishop K E Kirk.

I would read and study in the mornings; in the afternoons I would walk on the Yorkshire moors, or else be conscripted by Father Bell into gardening in the grounds. In the evenings I read mainly biographies, especially those of some leading Anglican teachers and pastors.

During this time at Mirfield I had the great privilege of taking part in a retreat conducted by Father Keble Talbot. It is impossible to convey the charm and attractiveness and vision of his addresses, but I am glad now that I jotted down these notes of some of his sayings:

There are whole bits of me that will not serve from love; then I must serve as a slave. What we cannot do out of love, we must do out of duty. If you cannot go uphill in top gear, go in slow. But do go.

Our Lord came not to put shackles on the body, but to take shackles off the soul.

People who have really influenced me have been those who have not tried to influence me.

Christ on the cross accomplished our redemption. But we must still put on Christ. We must endorse our baptism. We must die daily to sin. We must be disinfected of our egoism.

There is a record black with the signatures and red with the seals of those who have borne witness in the heavenly places that God is true.

There was much in the life at Mirfield that pulled me tremendously. But there were some things that caused me doubt and uncertainty. The superior at that time was Father Raymond Raynes. He seemed to have a much more 'Western' or Roman outlook than many of the earlier generations of Mirfield fathers. A man of considerable charm, he nevertheless had a very rigid, almost fanatical, viewpoint. I could not help wondering whether, under his leadership, the Community would become rather different from the CR I had known and loved. As things turned out eventually, I do not think I need have worried.

The other matter which I found perplexing was that the ministry of many of the fathers seemed largely involved with people who were already committed and keen Christians, eg the work of conducting retreats, acting as chaplains and visitors to women's communities and convents, counselling and giving spiritual direction to priests, nuns and the more devout laity. This work was undoubtedly vitally important, and of the greatest value to the Church, but I knew that I had been drawn to the work of a parish priest, one who tries to be a 'fisher of men' and who finds in his nets fish of all kinds.

When we got near to Holy Week one of the CR fathers, who had been asked to give the Holy Week addresses in a parish at

Middlesborough, was suddenly taken ill and could not go. I was asked to go in his place. Of course I was a poor substitute for a Mirfield father, but no doubt the hard-pressed vicar was thankful to have some extra help in a very busy week. After three months away from it all, I found it almost overwhelming to be back in the hum and throb of a very lively and active parish. We had well-attended services during Holy Week and a very happy and inspiring Easter Day.

But the following day, when I returned to Mirfield, my mind was in a turmoil. I do not think that the Community today would permit an aspirant to have this kind of interruption. After a few very troubled days, I saw the superior and told him that I could not ask to be made a novice. I left the House of the Resurrection the following morning, feeling very sad. But I shall always be most grateful to CR for their hospitality and kindness and for all that they taught me.

For some time I went through a very difficult period. I thought of the young man in the Gospel to whom our Lord said:

'If thou wilt be perfect, go and sell that thou hast, and give to the poor, and thou shalt have treasure in Heaven; and come and follow me.' And when the young man heard that saying, he went away sorrowful; for he had great possessions.

I wrote to the Bishop of Portsmouth, but he did not seem very interested. Perhaps he thought of me as a Mirfield reject and, anyhow, he did not look very sympathetically towards the Community of the Resurrection. At that time many bishops were trying to find livings for men who had been chaplains to the Forces and were hoping to return to parish life. So, although I had been in orders for twelve years, there was no offer to me of a benefice.

I was, however, offered a curacy in the large country parish of Stansted Mountfitchett, Essex. Most people think of Essex as a flat and uninteresting county. The western part, however, which includes the district round Stansted, consisted of delightful rolling countryside, with not a few hills, and it was one of the most abundant corn-growing areas in the country.

In the forties and fifties there were still many quite unspoiled little villages, with moated farmhouses, gracious manor houses, thatched cottages and large tranquil village greens, often over-looked by unrestored village inns and ancient parish churches. Only a few miles from Stansted there was Audley End, one of the greatest country houses in England, and there were also noble great churches like Thaxted and Saffron Walden. I did not have a car in those days, but I bought a bicycle and spent many happy hours roaming the comparatively car-free lanes and exploring the countryside. After five years in a very battered dockland area, it was bliss beyond words to unwind in the peace of the country.

My new vicar was one of the Church of England's wandering stars. Most Monday mornings he would leave his vicarage and drive post-haste to the cathedral city, Chelmsford. There he would be happily immersed, for most of the week, in the activi-ties of every possible (and impossible) diocesan committee. It seemed that it was only rarely that he visited his parishioners. On the whole he left to me this pastoral duty and the care of the sick and dying. I was very happy to try to undertake this work, for the parishioners, rich and poor, were most friendly and welcoming. The only embarrassment was that frequently I had to make excuses for the absence of my vicar.

Some families were especially hospitable and welcoming. One of the churchwardens was a local farmer who lived, with his wife and daughter, in a delightful old farmhouse which was surrounded by huge and ancient barns, some with outstandingly fine timber roofs. He farmed about 350 acres, growing mostly wheat and oats. He was a very keen member of the local hunt, the Essex Union. Every wood, covert and spinney for miles around was known to him, as he had hunted the country for many years. There would be no motorised horsebox for him; he would set out early for the meet, follow hounds all day (usually being in at the death) and would return home, perhaps miles away, in the evening, thoroughly tired but extremely contented.

But, however exhausted he was on the Saturday evening, he would never be absent from his place at 8 am Holy Communion on Sunday.

He was a splendid character, modest, quiet and generous, who was never known to speak evil of anyone. Physically he was very tough but, having not seen a doctor for many years, he dropped down dead one morning in his farmyard, from a massive heart attack. His only daughter took over the farm and ran it for over thirty years. Like her father, Susan was a loyal follower of the hunt and a keen supporter of the church.

I realised, while I was at Stansted, what a firm hold hunting has on the affections of the country people. The anti-hunting freaks are mainly town-bred folk with little knowledge or understanding of country ways. In recent years, the League Against Cruel Sports has bussed out from the towns coachloads of lager-louts and thugs, who have tried to disrupt the meets with violent and offensive behaviour. No doubt these folk are descendants of the Puritans, who tried to ban dancing and the maypole and theatres and even threw organs out of the churches.

While at Stansted I became much involved with youth work. We had a lively Youth Fellowship and I took over the running of the Scout troop. Although food rationing made it all very difficult, we had splendid annual camps. Our campsite was at Felbrigg Hall near West Runton, Norfolk. The owner, Mr R W Ketton-Cremer, the eminent historian, was a most generous host. He allowed us to camp amongst the beech trees adjoining Felbrigg Park and we would walk the three miles to the Norfolk coast, through cornfields ablaze with red poppies. On one occasion he showed us round his home a week after he had shown Queen Mary round the same rooms. This gracious house is now the property of the National Trust; I am thankful to have known it when it was still in private ownership.

But these few years after the war were difficult and disappointing ones. Rationing was more severe than it had been during the war. There were some unusually severe winters but coal was short and sometimes we had the electricity cut off. No doubt the Labour Government had severe problems but the people were disappointed and discontented with all the shortages and restrictions.

I had a wonderful break in the summer of 1946. To my great joy, I was invited to take holiday duty for a month at St John's, Territet, Montreux. It was still not very easy to get out of England and to escape from the frustration of wartime controls and red-tape. Weary hours had to be spent queuing for visas and exit permits at the London consulates, as thousands of others also longed to escape for a while from the austere prison of post-war Britain.

Never had the outward journey to Switzerland been more interesting. The docks and town of Calais were still in a very shattered state and every bridge on the line to Paris had been damaged by the RAF. It was a tremendous joy to reach Switzerland again: never did the 6 am coffee at the buffet at Vallorbe station taste better.

The stay in Montreux was like journeying backwards in time to recover a lost world; a world in which the shops were full, in which cakes were still made with real butter and real cream, and in which shopkeepers received their customers with courtesy and pleasure. There was still a little rationing in Switzerland that first year after the war, but compared with England it was a land flowing with milk and honey.

This holiday was memorable for my first visit to the High Alps of Canton Valais. I had visited Switzerland four times, and had spent two winters playing about in the snow, but until September 1946 I had never got near to the real Alpine giants. I had seen them – the 14,000-foot giants of the Pennine Alps – from afar, from the Rochers de Naye near Montreux, but I had never been to the high mountain canton of Valais and I had certainly never anticipated climbing there.

But my friends, the Petrie family from Les Avants, were leaving for a holiday at Zermatt and I was invited to spend a few days with them. So, having been given leave from my chaplaincy in midweek, I went with them.

The weather had been cloudy and overcast in the Rhône Valley but, as the little mountain train pulled into Zermatt station, the Matterhorn stood out free from cloud, its snow-sprinkled silhouette clear against the blue sky.

We had a few days of mountain-walks and family picnics, but soon bigger plans were being hatched. I was captivated by all the paraphernalia of the climbing game: the assembly of rucksacks, ropes, ice-axes, sun-goggles, gloves; the looking up at the heights and the planning of expeditions; the preparations for a night at a mountain hut and the buying of provisions.

I was egged on by the younger members of the Petrie family, but did not need much persuasion to join them on an expedition. I was given a morning's training on the Riffelhorn, by one of the Zermatt guides, and then pronounced passable to join their party for an expedition.

Incidentally, on my first climb practically everything I wore was lent by members of the Petrie family: boots, sweater, breeches, anorak and gloves – my underclothes were the only garments of my own.

Soon after this first expedition I had to return to Montreux for chaplaincy duties. But, later that month, I was again able to slip away for the inside of a week. Up till now, Montreux itself had been the limit of my hopes and ambitions, in its lovely setting on Lake Léman. But once I had tasted the joys of the High Alps, the clear mountain air, the peace of the high valleys remote from tourists and motor coaches, and the thrill of climbing together with good friends, I would never again be entirely content with lowland Switzerland.

So I was delighted to receive an invitation to join my old friend Sophie Tiarks, who was staying at Saas Fee, near Zermatt. Sophie had been a regular visitor to Saas Fee for over fifty years. Now, after the break of the war years, she was staying there again, with a friend, and they were re-visiting their many old friends in the village. Saas Fee then had not been developed as a skiing centre; there was no road or railway to the village and it remained as it had been for centuries, a delightful little Alpine village.

Soon after my arrival I was talking over, with a guide, what was to be my first real climb, the Portiengrat. We left our hotel in the village about 8 pm and walked up very fast to the mountain hut. It was a glorious moonlit night. As we climbed up the rocky path I looked across to the vast range of the Dom, its snowfield showing up clearly in the bright moonlight. We reached the hut about 11 pm, drank a bottle of wine and went to sleep for a few hours.

I liked my guide, Meinrad Burman, very much. He spoke English quite well and, on our walk up, told me thrilling stories of how he and other Swiss guides had helped, and guided down, English prisoners-of-war who had escaped from Italy over the mountains.

We started our climb before dawn. There was the usual misery (novel, then, for me) of being pulled out of my sleeping-bag by the guide, sleepily lacing up boots by candlelight, forcing down a few mouthfuls of food, then going out into freezing darkness. There followed hours of dull tramping up the moraine and the glacier, trying to follow in the flickering light of my guide's lantern.

As we reached the rocks there was the thrill of roping-up to begin the real ascent. Then the joy and exhilaration of climbing up into the sunshine; the pause for a second breakfast; the peeling off of sweaters and gloves and the satisfaction of a brief rest and a quick cigarette. How good life was! A perfect summer's day; splendid firm warm rock, a competent guide; enough excitement to make it a real adventure and the feeling that we were going to get to the top.

We reached the summit in reasonable time. Meinrad was in great form, yodelling like a schoolboy. On the summit there was one other party – a Swiss-German woman with her guide. The view was superb; even Meinrad had scarcely ever known it better. We could see all the northern Italian lakes, as well as the great circle of giant Alpine peaks, and we stayed over an hour on the top.

The descent from the summit was, to me, most terrifying. A smooth rock sloped down, just like the roof of a house. Meinrad doubled a rope round an iron stanchion and told me to walk backwards down the slab, pulling on the rope, for about forty-eight yards. It was easy for Meinrad to jeer: 'Stand up straight; lean back,' but behind me was a 5,000-foot drop and I was 13,000 feet up. However, when this pitch was concluded, we made a quick descent, glissading down the snow slopes which are a feature of this side of the mountain.

The walk back to Saas Fee was pure joy. We were victors and I had climbed my first real peak.

Soon this interlude in the High Alps was over and I returned to my duties at the English church at Montreux. It was a most happy experience to be conducting services again in the beautiful church of St John's, Territet, and to see once again old friends of the English colony. Some of them had remained there all through the war, marooned in a neutral island in the heart of wartime Europe. It was fascinating to hear their experiences.

I returned to Stansted, with a thankful heart, after a month's stay; my first real holiday for six years.

My ministry at Stansted lasted three and a half years. Despite the beauty of the countryside and the friendship of our parishioners, these were very difficult and disappointing years. No doubt, like many people in England, I was still tired and drained by the stress of the war years and, although the Labour Government had great problems to face, most folk were completely disenchanted by their attempted solutions and angry about the continuing shortages and restrictions and government regulations.

But there were some bright moments during this rather bleak and difficult period of my life. Only the other day I received a letter from someone I had known then: a young soldier stationed at Stansted with whom I had completely lost touch for over forty years.

There was an army camp at Stansted for young National Service recruits and, for some years, I was a part-time officiating chaplain there. I used to conduct Padre's Hours and short services and this young soldier played the piano for hymns. As he seemed lonely and depressed, I used, sometimes, to invite him back to my lodgings for a meal and a chat.

After I left Stansted, we drifted apart. He later went to Cambridge, became ordained, got married, produced two children, had a distinguished career and is now on the verge of retiring from his present post as residentiary canon at one of our cathedrals. The letter which I received the other day was to thank me for the help and friendship I gave him all those years ago which, apparently, meant a great deal to him at a difficult turning point in his life. 'Cast thy bread upon the waters for thou shalt find it after many days.'

However, I was troubled and uncertain about my own future, so it was not only a complete surprise to me, but also a great joy, when a letter dropped through my letter-box asking me if I would like to be considered as chaplain of Bryanston School. It came just as I was about to set off to run another summer camp at Felbrigg Park. But, as soon as the camp was over, I kept an appointment in London with the headmaster and the head of Cranborne Chase School for Girls.

This was soon followed by a long weekend at the school. I felt very much like an article sent on approval, as I was entertained in the homes of various housemasters and senior members of the staff who were, presumably, vetting me. At the end of the visit, I had a long interview with the headmaster. He was such a vague and unassuming man that, at the end of it, I was not sure whether I was being offered the appointment or not. But I rather thought I was.

After my return to Stansted, a letter came from the bursar, asking whether I could commence my duties at the beginning of January 1949. The subject of my salary was never mentioned by the head or the bursar, or anyone else, and I only found out what it was when I had been there for some weeks.

It was sad, in many ways, to say goodbye to friends at Stansted but the grief of separation was not as severe as it had been when I left previous parochial appointments.

As things turned out, I kept in fairly close touch with the parish for several years as, during the long school holidays, I returned there often and, for several years, continued to organise and run the annual Scout camp at Felbrigg Park.

I found that, after a term spent with the somewhat privileged youths of Bryanston, it was a good change to be back with the sons of farm labourers and agricultural workers.

5
Switzerland
1938–1940

O ye Mountains and Hills, bless ye the Lord:
praise Him and magnify Him for ever.

Benedicite

In August 1938 I took up my appointment as assistant chaplain at St John's, Territet, Montreux.

Until 1939 Montreux was almost like an English colony. Many English folk had settled there and some were living in pleasant villas which their families had owned since Victorian days. There were an English club, an English library, a golf club and two Anglican churches: one High and one Low.

The Low Church, at Clarens, was controlled by a society which was then known as the Colonial and Continental Church Society. This organisation, which was rather narrowly evangelical, had built and maintained a number of English churches on the Continent, many of them only maintained as seasonal chaplaincies, though Christ Church, Clarens, had a permanent chaplain.

St John's, Territet, had been built, and was kept going, by a local committee and was not under the thumb of any partisan society. The committee not only found the salary of the chaplain, but also paid a slightly higher salary to the full-time organist; in addition they were prepared to take me on as assistant chaplain, with special responsibility for the English boys and girls who were at schools around the Lake of Geneva.

One rather unusual, and very interesting, educational establishment was the Institute Fisher, Territet. This was owned, and controlled by, a remarkable Anglo-Indian woman, Miss Fisher. The school thrived on boys and girls who had been expelled from English public schools. It was bilingual and multinational.

Miss Fisher also had a lucrative connection with many presidents and wealthy businessmen from South American republics. The only snag about the politicians and presidents was that often, after she had accepted their children, there would be a revolution in their home republics, with the parents either assassinated or imprisoned. Miss Fisher would be left to maintain the children, without any money coming in, sometimes for years.

One of the more interesting students there in my time was Bobby Peel, son of Sir Robert Peel and Beatrice Lillie. His career at a top English public school had been abruptly ended and he tended to pay scant attention to school rules at the Institute Fisher. He kept a fast sports car at a nearby garage and was in the habit of climbing out of a window at night and driving, with a few chosen friends, to a night club in Lausanne. Bobby joined the Royal Navy when war broke out and was later killed in action.

I became very fond of Miss Fisher and would often drop in to listen with her to BBC radio, as the international news became monthly more menacing. She was very kind to the chaplain, who was a lonely and very nervous soul, and when, later, he became very ill, she nursed him devotedly.

A rather more orthodox English boarding school was Chillon College, which had been founded near the Château de Chillon, by the lake, and had later moved to Glion, a little village 1,000 feet above Territet. The English and American boys at this school were largely the sons of diplomats or businessmen who lived and worked in Europe, plus a scattering of youngsters whose families lived in the Far East or India.

I was also chaplain to St George's School, an exceptionally fine girls' boarding school at Clarens. Every Sunday about sixty of their girls came by tram to attend our services at Territet – and I went to Clarens for confirmation classes.

I also went, every week, to Chatelard School, a bigger school for girls, which had been established in what had been a big hotel at Les Avants. Both St George's and Chatelard were normal

English boarding schools, not finishing schools. They prepared youngsters for the English A levels and university entrance exams.

Altogether, there must have been about 400 English boys and girls at school in the area and, in June 1939, I presented about thirty-five of them for confirmation.

As we moved into November 1938, I became aware of a curious air of restlessness and expectancy among the boys at Chillon College. They were awaiting the coming of the snow. In a normal winter the slopes above Glion and Caux would be covered by snow between the beginning of December and the end of March. Whereas, in an English public school, the afternoons would be given to rugby or hockey or athletics, at Chillon the whole school would be out skiing once the snow had arrived. There was a little funicular railway which crept up the mountain between Glion and the Rochers de Naye. When snow conditions were favourable, they would run a shuttle service from Glion up the mountain. All the boys had season tickets and they were able to make quite a number of runs down during the afternoon.

The school was kind enough to give me a season ticket too, so, on many afternoons, I was able to join them in skiing. Having not long recovered from a serious spinal graft, I was at first rather worried that, if I fell, I might damage my back. I asked the local doctor whether, in the circumstances, it was all right to ski. He advised me not to, so I wrote home to my doctor in England. His advice was also negative, so I aimed higher up and consulted the specialist. When he also cautioned me against it, I felt the only thing to do was to go ahead and get started.

After about four months of regular skiing, my back was so improved that I have never had any trouble since. It was not the coming down on fast pistes that benefited my health. But Caux-Glion was not a fashionable centre and ski-lifts there were unknown. We did a lot of our skiing in deep powder-snow and then had to climb up again, herring-bone pattern, on our skis.

It was this hard work climbing up which so built up my back muscles that all the old pain was cured.

Some of the boys became very expert and one at least, in later years, represented England in international skiing events. My standard of skiing was, of course, very poor in comparison with theirs but by the end of the season I was able to get about with reasonable confidence. In those days few people worried about ski classes or professional teachers but, instead, gradually picked up the sport by watching more experienced and more skilful friends.

I shall always be grateful for those afternoons in the sun and snow on the Caux banks, looking across to the mountains of Savoy on the other side of the Lake of Geneva.

There were some very interesting people among the adult congregation of St John's.

Miss Gabrielle Lomas was one of the churchwardens. Her father was one of those responsible for building the church and I believe he gave the organ, as he himself was a keen organist. Gabrielle Lomas had lived there all her long life, in a delightful villa with big gardens overlooking the lake. Alas, today the site is occupied by a monstrous block of flats. She was tall and gracious and friendly; charming not only in appearance but in personality. She was also devout and a great supporter of the Anglican Church in Europe.

Mrs Alice Fawcus was one of the church's most faithful supporters. Her husband had been, for years, in business in Genoa, importing coal from South Wales. He became very rich but, during the First World War, he had developed TB. They went to Switzerland so that he could receive treatment and he died there. His widow stayed on and remained in Switzerland for the rest of her life. She had never been back to England since leaving it as a young bride many years before. Her home was a delightful large chalet at Blonay, above Vevey. She was very rich and had no children and few relatives, but she put her money to good use.

It was her habit to listen in, every Sunday, to the good cause appeal on BBC radio. On Monday morning she would sit down and write a cheque. But this was not the limit of her help. Often she would write a personal letter to the charity involved and frequently developed a friendship with its workers. Throughout the year she had a constant stream of visitors from England to stay with her; matrons, district nurses, social workers, slum priests and their families and other folk who she felt deserved a holiday in Switzerland, all expenses paid. Over the years she formed a large family of those who had been her guests. She slept badly but as she lay awake she would, for hours, intercede for them by name.

After breakfast, it was her invariable habit to spend two to three hours at the desk in her study, writing letters to the many folk she had befriended all over the world. In the afternoons she would be taken out in an ancient Daimler, driven slowly by an old retainer and accompanied by the guests who, at that period, were staying with her.

She was very kind to me and I loved her dearly, having learned to respect the disciplined way in which she extended her hospitality.

The doyenne of the English colony was the redoubtable Mrs Pym, who had lived for years in one of the hotels. She was then in her nineties but, on one occasion, I was a member of a party which she led up to the grassy summit of the Gramont, 9,000 feet high, on the other side of the lake. The expedition involved spending a night at a rather primitive inn. Next morning she was scrambling about like a chamois in the mountain meadows, which were covered with wild flowers – about which she was an expert. During the war she bossed-up the women of Montreux with firm discipline and had them knitting warm sweaters and stockings for the men of the Merchant Navy.

The church had a very faithful server and sacristan who motored over each Sunday from Vevey, where he had, for years, conducted a thriving dental practice. He was a very ardent Anglo-Catholic and was always goading the clergy into more extreme High Church practices. As a boy in England, when he had been prepared for confirmation, he had been taught about going to Confession when needed, but he had never made his Confession. One day I received a telephone call, asking me to go and visit him in hospital at Vevey, as he wanted to make his Confession. He died a few days later, but I was always thankful that I had heard his first Confession and that he had remembered the teaching he had been given sixty years before.

One of our most interesting parishioners was a man who had spent most of his life as an officer in the Indian Army and who was then transferred to be a commissioner of police. For some reason he had missed being confirmed at his school; now, as he was approaching the end of his journey, he sought the sacramental help of his church and asked me to prepare him for confirmation. As he was a somewhat formal character, he always dressed for dinner in his hotel and our weekly instruction class took place a short while after dinner. It was the first time I had taken a confirmation class for a candidate dressed in dinner jacket and black tie. The instruction was usually followed by his giving me a generous peg of whisky.

Perhaps my best friends at Territet were the Petrie family, who lived at Les Avants, above Montreux, in a house which, after they had moved back to England, they sold to Noël Coward.

Walter Petrie had made his fortune as an exporter from India and when he retired he went to live in Switzerland, as he could not face the English climate. His wife Violet was an exceedingly motherly woman who was always befriending and entertaining lame ducks. Shortly before I went to Montreux their eldest son went out to India, to take up an appointment. One day a cable arrived to say he had been taken ill; the following day another cable came to say he had died of a sudden infection. A few months later their second daughter, a beautiful and charming girl, was on a visit to friends in India. The same thing happened: news came that she had been taken ill and, almost at once, she died. Their oldest daughter, Poppy, had grown up in Switzerland. She was a fearless and skilled climber and also an experienced skier. The youngest child was a schoolboy at Chillon.

This was the family who, despite their grief, gave me a warm welcome into the family circle. Later they introduced me to the joys of mountain-walking and climbing. My first tentative attempts at skiing were made from their home.

When war came, Poppy would have loved to return to England to undertake some war work. But, with her parents still bowed down with grief, she was persuaded to stay with them and spent the whole war in Switzerland, rather cut off from friends of her own type and generation.

I was given a short holiday after Easter 1939, as the youngsters from the schools were all on vacation. I decided to take the train from Montreux through the Simplon Tunnel and on to Florence. As a companion, I took with me a Chillon boy who had been left on his own for the holidays and did not quite know what to do with himself.

We left Montreux on Easter Monday. Mussolini had invaded Albania on Good Friday and many people thought that the war was about to erupt. Our train from Montreux was almost empty as we approached the frontier, but every train we passed coming from Italy was crammed to the doors with English, Americans and others, trying to escape from Fascism before the war started. We also passed a number of troop trains full of Italian soldiers, and trucks laden with guns and tanks.

In the streets of Milan and Florence, seven men out of ten seemed to be in uniform. It was a strange atmosphere for my first visit to Florence. Every evening we reported to the British Legation to ask if they thought it safe to stay another day. Nevertheless, I was enchanted and intoxicated by the loveliness of Florence and vowed to return as soon as possible in happier days; a vow which I was fortunate enough to keep after the war.

We had some happy days exploring the streets and art galleries and churches, then my companion received a telegram from his parents, instructing him to leave Italy at once. We hopped back over the frontier, to Lugano, where we spent the remaining days of our Easter break. Although it was not Italy, we were surrounded by Italian architecture and even the Italian language, as well as the beauty of the lake.

During the next few months the war clouds darkened. Everyone in Switzerland was convinced that war was coming and could not understand why England seemed so heedless of approaching events. Travellers coming through from Germany all spoke of the roads being blocked by troops on the move and endless lines of tanks and guns.

We had glorious weather that last summer of peace. The youngsters from the schools went on swimming and boating on the lake and playing tennis and enjoying picnics. Our generation became increasingly concerned, as we read our papers and listened, each night, to the broadcasts.

When I returned to England, at the beginning of the school holidays in July, I realised it was most unlikely that I would be returning to Montreux and left with a heavy heart.

When war broke out, the children who had returned to England for the holidays did not go back to their Swiss schools and I was left without a job. I was offered a temporary curacy on the staff of All Hallows-by-the-Tower and lived and worked there until Christmas.

The City of London was an interesting place from which to see the beginnings of the Second World War. It was the period of the phoney war. Everyone had expected that London would be heavily bombed as soon as the war began, but nothing much happened to the city all that winter. However, preparations had been made and all possible precautions undertaken. A chain of Civil Defence installations had been set up in the City; casualty-clearing centres and First Aid posts, ARP centres, depots for workers ready to repair the roads and water mains, demolition squads and fire fighters.

All these men, totalling several hundred, had to remain on duty and not leave their posts for several days and nights on end. As they were living rough, in improvised quarters, they had little to do and became exceedingly bored. All Hallows was about the only City church whose clergy actually lived in their parish. So we felt we had a special ministry to these unwilling wartime parishioners, wherever they were billeted in the City – within our parish boundaries and beyond. To relieve their boredom, we took round dartboards, packs of cards, magazines and books, to help them get through the hours of inactivity.

Before long we were conducting evening singsongs, which became very popular. My friend Father George Moore was a skilled player of his piano-accordion. Although a lover of classical music, he had a vast repertoire of music-hall songs, the old favourites of the First World War and the current popular music. He said, after a few months, that if he put his squeeze-box down it would start playing, on its own, songs like 'Lily of Laguna', 'Pack up your Troubles', 'Down Mexico Way' and 'Roll Out the Barrel'.

Before long we were asked to conduct short services on Sunday evenings at these ARP centres. Night after night Father Moore and I would grope our way through the blackout to visit our out-stations, he staggering under the weight of his heavy piano-accordion while I carried, in a rucksack, a supply of hymn books and carol sheets. One of the most enthusiastic audiences for our musical evenings was the large emergency hospital which had been set up in the basement of the P & O head office in Leadenhall Street.

I have conducted short services in practically all the fire stations in the City. One of these, in Aldgate, was manned almost entirely by Jewish firemen. Before going there, I had carefully thought out hymns which did not contain any reference to Christ, in order to avoid offending their religious susceptibilities (eg such hymns as 'God of Bethel' and 'Guide Me, O Thou Great Redeemer'). On one occasion, when we had finished a little early, I asked them if they would like to choose a hymn to sing. From the back a hand went up and the request came: 'Please can we have "Onward Christian Soldiers".'

On another occasion, I was conducting a service in a recreation room on the first floor of a fire station. Suddenly the fire bell went. At once my entire congregation slid down the pole in the middle of the room and I was left alone with the woman who had come with me to accompany the hymns on a portable organ.

But the most curious and romantic centre to visit was Trig Wharf, down by the Thames near Blackfriars. It was an eerie place to visit in the blackout on a dark night, sited beside the inky waters of the Thames. Here, kept in readiness, were about eighty navvies, rough types, ready to repair the roads and sewers and water mains. They did not take kindly to being cooped up for several days on end, as it was against regulations for them to go out, even to the nearest pub – though they managed to have copious supplies of liquor brought in. Our singsongs there were remarkably beery and cheery.

One of the curates at All Hallows was a very skilled card player. He would visit Trig Wharf at night and spend hours playing poker. Owing to his great ability at playing cards, he would win a considerable sum of money. For this, he was held in great reverence by the navvies and he seemed to be able to hold them in the palm of his hand. At the end of the session, he would say, 'Men, it is now time for our night prayers.' They would stand up in a large circle and he would get them to repeat after him, line by line, the sort of very simple prayers which would normally be thought suitable for a kindergarten class.

During this period we did not see much of our vicar, the Reverend Tubby Clayton, as he had gone up to Scapa Flow to organise a Toc H club for the fleet. But his curates became well known in ARP circles all round the City. It was a curious initiation to the war but, later on, I found this experience most useful in our ministry amongst the air-raid centres in Portsmouth.

Towards the end of December, I received a telegram from the churchwardens at St John's Territet, asking me if I would go out for a few months to take charge of the church, as the chaplain had fallen and broken his leg. With some difficulty, I obtained permission to undertake this wartime journey. I left London on Boxing Day, 1939. We crossed from Dover to Calais in a ferry without lights. The blackout in Paris was as rigorous as that of London. I caught the train to Montreux and was amazed, that night, to walk about in a city with all the lights blazing out.

It was delightful to conduct services again in St John's, albeit with a much reduced congregation and a great absence of youngsters.

Montreux was an interesting place during the months of the phoney war, as it was a great centre for spies of all nations. One of our congregation at the English church worked in the travel department of the local branch of the Thomas Cook tourist agency. He was, therefore, well placed to keep tabs on the arrivals and departures of many interesting foreigners and was able to pass on useful information to our Secret Service.

It was a great joy to me to be able to get in some skiing again. Without any foreign visitors, the skiing slopes were strangely empty. Sometimes the only people one met on skis were Swiss army patrols having their winter training.

A very happy memory of this time is of a cross-country tour on skis, sleeping in mountain huts. I was invited to join a small group by Poppy Petrie; it was an international group, including a couple of youngsters. We climbed up the snow slopes with skins on our skis, each carrying a rucksack containing provisions for a few days.

When we reached the mountain hut above Saanen, we had to dig the snow away from the door to get in. Once inside, we found the pile of firewood and the blankets with which the Swiss Alpine Club stocked their huts and we soon had the fire going and had melted snow into our dixies to boil up some hot soup. We had a delightful circular tour which finished up, I think, at Zeiswimmen.

By the time we reached Easter, the chaplain had recovered from his broken leg and I was making plans to return to England.

Soon after the war had broken out, I had tried to obtain an army chaplaincy but, as soon as the doctors had learned of my medical history, I was turned down without question. While I was pondering what the next chapter would be, a letter arrived from my old college friend the Reverend Archie Franklin. He had been senior curate at St Mary's, Portsea, before leaving to take up a parochial appointment in Leeds. He suggested my name to Canon Robins, who was searching for staff as several curates from his vast parish had left for wartime services with the Forces. So I was offered, and I accepted, the post of priest-in-charge of St Wilfrid's, in the parish of St Mary, Portsea.

I said my goodbyes to the church folk at Territet, wondering whether I would ever see them again or officiate again in their delightful church.

Just at that time the German invasion of the Low Countries began. There were day-long queues and people sleeping all night outside our consulate at Lausanne as worried English folk tried to secure the necessary authorisations to travel. Fortunately I knew a typist who worked at the legation. I gave her my passport, which was returned that night, duly stamped.

I caught the night train to Paris and Calais, which was one of the last trains to get through before the Germans invaded France.

6

Chingford
1933–1938

Try as he will, no man breaks wholly loose
From his first love, no matter who she be.
Oh was there ever sailor free to choose,
That didn't settle somewhere near the sea? . . .
Parsons in pulpits, taxpayers in pews,
Kings on your thrones, you know as well as me,
We've only one virginity to lose,
And where we lost it there our hearts will be!

Rudyard Kipling

On St Thomas's Day (21 December) 1933, I was ordained deacon to serve in the parish of St Peter and St Paul, Chingford, Essex. The Bishop of Chelmsford had decided, that year, to hold the ordination at the cathedral-like parish church of Thaxted. I was, of course, delighted that the service should be in such a beautiful setting. Thaxted church, with its tall spire seen from miles away across the surrounding countryside and with its beautiful interior, light, airy and spacious, is one of the finest of the many fine churches in East Anglia.

Conrad Noel had then been vicar for twenty-three years and he was now sixty-four and had become nearly blind. The grandson of Lord and Lady Gainsborough, he had had a privileged childhood but, after he was ordained, he became one of the Church's stormiest petrels and most controversial priests. He had found it exceedingly difficult to be ordained, as no bishop seemed to accept him. This was partly because of his ardent work for the Christian Socialist cause and partly because he was connected with some very extreme ritualistic churches. He was far too much of a firebrand for any bishop to ordain. For some time he stumped the country, lecturing and speaking on behalf of Christian Socialism.

Some years later, when he had accepted a curacy at Paddington Green, he became very interested in the somewhat bohemian life of Fleet Street and the West End theatres and music halls. He made friends with a number of men who subsequently became famous, including G K Chesterton, Hilaire Belloc, George Bernard Shaw, Augustus John and William Orpen.

Later he worked in the parish of St Mary's, Primrose Hill, where Percy Dearmer developed the splendid ceremonial of the pre-Reformation Church of England. For years Dearmer was the leading exponent of English Use, fully Catholic worship and teaching, but according to the Use of Sarum and not at all like the contemporary style of Roman Catholic churches. It was this kind of dignified and restrained worship that Conrad Noel later introduced at Thaxted, although the incense and processions and English vestments and servers' albs came as a shock to the Essex villagers.

In 1910 the Countess of Warwick, who had the patronage, presented Conrad Noel to the benefice of Thaxted. After the First World War he became known nationally through the 'Battle of the Flags'. He had placed a Sinn Fein flag and a Red Flag in the church. For many weekends, groups of undergraduates would come from Cambridge and try to remove these flags and replace them with the Union Jack. Sometimes there were scuffles and some disorder.

But all the turmoil had died down by the time of my ordination and Conrad himself had mellowed. When he died, the very conservative and devout evangelical, Bishop Henry Wilson of Chelmsford, paid an affectionate tribute to him at his Memorial Service, saying:

> I believe it to be literally true that he was the greatest personality among the clergy in this diocese, as a student, as a writer, as a religious and political leader, as a man of artistic and musical sense, and most of all, as a saint of God. . . . His courage, which

was unbounded, remained to the end, and as he lived so he died, a brave and faithful servant of Jesus Christ.

I have always been grateful that my ministry began in the beautiful and inspiring surroundings of Thaxted and many times, since, I have returned in thankful pilgrimage.

Until the early years of this century, Chingford had been a quiet little Essex village on the fringe of Epping Forest. Between the wars there was a great amount of building, mainly by private enterprise but there was also a large LCC housing estate. In my first years in the parish it seemed that whole streets of little suburban houses would spring up in the green fields overnight. We tried to visit the new arrivals, to welcome them to the parish, but it was hard work to keep up.

The parish was served by a vicar and three curates; in addition to the large Victorian parish church there was Chingford Old Church (which had been saved from being a picturesque old ruin and beautifully restored); also a mission church. It was a good training parish, as there were a number of keen, committed layfolk and much useful activity.

I started a Youth Fellowship and also took over the Scout troop. The system on which it was run had been learned during my time with the Lord Mayor's Own troop in the City of London. I asked a lot from the boys who joined. They were expected to clock up five attendances a week: troop night on Fridays; open-air scouting on Saturday afternoon; attendance at the Sung Eucharist on Sunday mornings; an informal Scouts' Own (or Bible class) on Sunday afternoons and a patrol meeting arranged by the patrol leader one evening a week. It was asking a great deal of the boys and I do not think the modern generation would be willing to give up so much time. There was, of course, no TV then and few parents had cars. There were not many outings, as the boys were not given much pocket-money. At any rate, the system seemed to work. The troop must have meant quite a lot to that generation for, nearly sixty years later, some of the members come to see me, bringing with them their children and grandchildren.

When I first went to Chingford, I lived in digs. But there were soon complaints from my landlady about the number of callers. One day I saw that there was a flat to let over the row of shops opposite the parish church. I took the flat and it became a home for curates for the next fifteen years or more.

The flat was on the first floor, over a greengrocer's shop, and it soon became known as Greengrocery Grange. I had a splendid large sitting-room facing the church, with a bedroom adjacent, and also a small kitchen and bathroom. Downstairs, behind the shop, there was a large room which we converted into a Scout headquarters. For the rest of my stay in Chingford I was seldom alone in the flat.

My year as a deacon was interrupted by illness. For months I had been troubled by back pain and, increasingly, the sciatic nerve all down my left thigh had given constant pain, especially at nights. I had been to several consultants and specialists, as well as to an osteopath. I had been massaged and manipulated, given exercises, stretched and hung up on a wall, but all to no effect.

Eventually I got in touch with St Luke's Hospital for the Clergy, in Fitzroy Square, London. This splendid institution was the gift of the medical profession to the clergy, inasmuch as the Harley Street consultants on whose services they could call did not charge for their work. I saw Mr St John Buxton, a leading orthopaedic surgeon. After several interviews and X-rays, he advised a spinal operation.

This involved sawing off a strip of bone from my shinbone and grafting it in as a splint in my spine. He had diagnosed my trouble as traumatic arthritis, caused by a blow sustained while playing football. The effect of the operation would be that two lower lumbar vertebrae would be fused together. At that time the operation was rare, but Mr Buxton assured me that there was a good chance of it being successful, as the previous man on whom he had performed the operation was a coal-heaver who was now back at work.

The operation was performed at St Luke's in October 1933.

They had prepared, beforehand, a large plaster shell which stretched from my neck to my knees, closely shaped to my body. It had been made rather like a chocolate egg, in two halves. When I had to be given a blanket bath, the top half would be lifted up while I was washed; then it was replaced and I was rolled over so that the back half could be lifted up and my back washed. I remained flat on my back in this contraption from October until February, able only to raise my head a little. The nursing staff were wonderfully kind and efficient and it was, I think, largely their ministrations which brought me through a difficult period.

On Christmas Day the nurses put on a little revue in a down-stairs lounge and most of the patients were wheeled down to see it. As I could not be moved, the cast came up and performed their song and dance routine in my room.

My parishioners, and other friends in London, were wonder-fully kind and there were few days when I did not have after-noon visitors. When my stay at St Luke's was over, I still had to have some weeks' convalescence. Then I was advised to seek an easier job, preferably a cushy parish on the south coast. But, being young and foolish, I opted to return to the busy life of Chingford parish and the chaotic racket of Greengrocery Grange.

I have always remembered one incident which occurred during my illness. It happened while I was under the anaes-thetic during the operation. I was aware of being in great, almost unbearable, pain. But it was made perfectly clear to me that this was right and necessary and that all would be well. I read in the Good Book: 'It was good for me to have been in trouble.'

Looking back, I see clearly that I was allowed to learn more in my time at St Luke's than I had ever learned in a theological college.

It is interesting to recollect the change in the value of money.

As a curate of Chingford, I was paid the salary of £180 a year. On this I managed to pay the rent for my flat, pay for my food, clothes and incidental expenses – and even afford a fortnight's holiday.

But goods were remarkably cheap. While at Chingford, I bought an evening dress suit with a reasonably well-cut dinner jacket and trousers, for the sum of £2.10s.0d. at the Fifty-Shilling Tailors. Thomas Cook were offering a fortnight's holiday in Switzerland, including fare, for £10.

I met some interesting people during the years at Chingford. One was Ernest Raymond, who had achieved fame and fortune from the best-selling war novel *Tell England*. He was an old friend of my rector and came to give a lecture to mark the opening of our new church hall.

During my years at Chingford, my rector resigned. During the interregnum, one of my colleagues, who was curate-in-charge of our mission church, wrote to the wife of Winston Churchill, inviting her to come and open the church bazaar. Winston, at that time, was our local MP, Chingford being part of the constituency of Epping. My colleague wrote on printed parish notepaper and Clemmie probably thought she was being asked to open a big bazaar in one of the principal towns in her husband's constituency, so she consented to come.

On the day of the bazaar my colleague was taken ill and I was deputed to receive Mrs Churchill in his stead. I felt deeply ashamed and embarrassed as, in fact, the sale was being held in a rather miserable little hut with a tin roof and the bazaar was only the effort of a small mission congregation; it consisted of a few rather pathetic stalls. The day was very miserable, with a thick fog. Nevertheless, Mrs Churchill set out from Chartwell and her car crawled through the London traffic. However disappointed she must have been at the scene when she arrived, she did not show it. Instead, she was perfectly charming and declared the bazaar open in a humorous little speech. Later, as I gave her tea at a rickety little card table, I marvelled at her good humour and friendliness. She certainly scored a good mark in my book that day.

As the months went on, the pain in my sciatic nerve increased and I began to realise I would never regain fitness and health if I remained in Chingford. One day, in June 1937, a letter dropped through the letter-box onto the mat of my Chingford flat. It came from a woman whom I had never met and of whom I had never heard. She told me that she had heard of my continued pain and would like to send me a cheque, to enable me to consult Dr Rollier, of Leysin in Switzerland.

The letter was from Mrs Alice Fawcus, of Blonay. As I learned subsequently, she had heard of my plight through Father Moore, of All Hallows-by-the-Tower. A few weeks later I travelled out for an interview with Dr Rollier.

Leysin was on a sunny shelf, facing south, above the Rhône Valley. At the top of the mountain a number of hospitals and sanatoria had been established for the treatment of folk ill with TB lung disease, as it had been thought that the clear mountain air would help towards a cure. A little lower down the mountain were the clinics established by Dr Rollier.

He had acquired an international reputation for the treatment of tubercular bone disease. He was a fanatical believer in the power and efficacy of the sun's rays in curing this dread illness. His system consisted mainly in putting his patients on beds on the many south-facing balconies. Here they would lie flat for months, and sometimes years. Each day, for six hours or more, they would be stretched out, reclining on their stomachs with their backs bare to the sun's rays. As the air at that height was so clear and the sun's rays so hot, patients would begin with only two minutes at a time exposed to the sun, but this would be increased until they spent practically all the daylight hours, summer and winter alike, lying bare in the sun. Those who had been there for some months became so brown that they might have been taken as Africans.

Dr Rollier gave me a careful examination and concluded that a stay of two or three months in his clinic would be of great benefit to my condition, even though I had not got TB bones.

He had a somewhat jaundiced view of British doctors and their reliance on drugs. 'Ze British', he would say, 'are ze walking drug stores.' All drugs were banned from his clinics, as were all condiments, as well as alcohol and tobacco; he also prescribed special diets, mainly vegetarian. In the end I was given three months' leave of absence by my parish and returned to Leysin in August to be under Dr Rollier's care.

The clinic I was in was rather like a very comfortable Swiss hotel. It must have been very expensive but, as the fees were being paid by Mrs Fawcus, I had no financial worries.

Nearby was a large *clinique manufactoire* for working-class men, mainly Swiss and German. The long wards, also open to the sun, had overhead looms, with a leather belt running down beside each bed to power machinery on a bedside table. While lying prone, the patients, some of whom were staying for years, would work away at watch-making or some other craft, thus overcoming monotony and enabling them to earn some money.

There was also a delightful children's clinic. I saw photographs there of children who had arrived with terribly crippled and deformed legs and backs; next were pictures of the same children taken, perhaps, two years later, completely cured by the sun treatment, with limbs straight and bronzed, ready at the end to play and jump about in the snow.

This clinic so impressed me that, years later, when I was on the staff at Bryanston, I recommended it strongly to help the little daughter of one of my colleagues. She suffered very severely from asthma. Her mother and father agreed to her going out to receive treatment from Dr Rollier. I took her out myself, a somewhat formidable task for a bachelor parson to take out a little girl of ten on the long train journey (we did not fly in those days). I had hoped that she would sleep during the long night journey from Paris to the station for Leysin. Instead, she sat up and demanded to play noughts and crosses with me all night. I felt a brute at leaving her behind in the clinic, as she spoke no French and none of the children or the nurses in her ward could speak a word of English. Nine months later, I visited her again. By then she had forgotten her English words and greeted me with, '*Bonjour, M le Curé.*' Her asthma was almost completely cured and I do not think she suffered much with it afterwards. This happy incident with Jane took place about ten years after my own first visit to Leysin.

My own stay as a patient at Leysin lasted from August until nearly Christmas 1937. From my bed on our sunny balcony I looked out across the Rhône Valley to the far-off mountains of Valais. The time passed quickly enough, with reading and writing letters; also, sometimes, I was allowed up and could visit other patients and talk with them; especially I enjoyed visiting the children's clinic.

By December I was considerably better and free from pain. Once again I returned to my parish which I had learned to love so much. But, during 1938, I began to go downhill in health again and I was told that I would never be really well unless I left Chingford for a less demanding parish.

Once again, out of the blue, a surprise letter arrived at my flat. It was from the Reverend Martin Evans, chaplain of St John's, Territet, Montreux, asking me if I would join him as assistant chaplain.

He was a very good and devoted priest, but felt quite unable to understand, or cope with, the hundreds of young people in the educational establishments around Montreux. This time I felt it was right to accept.

'There is no parish like one's first parish,' so I left Chingford at the end of August, feeling terribly sorry to leave and wondering if I should ever be happy again.

It was a curious moment to begin my work at Territet. I arrived at about the same time as Mr Chamberlain visited Munich. War seemed likely to break out at any time and I half wondered whether it was worth unpacking my bags.

However, the tension eased somewhat and I began to settle down to what became an exceedingly happy year, lived against a background of darkening skies and increasing fears of war.

7

The City of London
1922–1933

> ... he hath shewed me marvellous great kindness
> in a strong city.
>
> Psalm 31. 21

In January 1992 I began work in the City of London. As I had
not obtained any qualifications in my schooldays, I had looked
for a job in the Situations Vacant column in the *Daily Telegraph*.
I answered an advertisement seeking a junior clerk (a euphemism for office boy) in a shipping company in Fenchurch Street.

I secured the post, but after a month I was given the sack. It
was the first, and only, time that I have been sacked, but it was
a very salutary experience for me. The reasons given were that
I had wasted too much time dawdling, when sent on errands,
and that I could not add up correctly: I had been given a very
long column of figures (£.s.d.) to add and had arrived at a wrong
total.

Shortly afterwards I secured a similar job, this time with an
old-established firm of timber brokers in Clements Lane, a
narrow turning off Lombard Street. My salary for the first year
was 15s. a week. My father paid for my season ticket from our
home to Liverpool Street and also bought my clothes. Apart
from this, I had to manage on my salary. But living was cheap
and I used to have an excellent lunch for 1s.6d. – roast joint and
two vegetables for 1s. 2d. plus hot pudding for 4d.

The firm who employed me did not, themselves, own a single
piece of timber; their considerable business was all done on
paper, selling timber on commission. The softwoods department
sold wood for ARCOS, the Soviet exporters, and the annual sales
realised millions of pounds. I was taken on by the hardwoods
department. This handled wood from all over the world: oak

and ash lumber from the United States, beech from Czechoslovakia, teak from Burma, *okoume* and other native woods from
West Africa, plywood from Finland and, most interesting of all,
great squared mahogany logs from Belize, British Honduras.

These last were landed at West India Docks, where they could
be inspected and then sold at monthly auctions in the City,
which were attended by buyers from all over the world. It was
not long since auctions had been conducted 'by the light of the
candle': a lighted candle was placed on the auctioneer's rostrum
and a pin placed near the top of the candle; the last bid received
before the pin fell out secured the particular lot on offer. By the
time I arrived at the firm, the auctions were conducted in
the modern way, but they were still great occasions, when
hundreds of thousands of pounds changed hands, and they
formed a considerable part of the firm's income.

My employers must have been one of the most old-fashioned
firms in the City. They were not a limited company, but a private
partnership, with eight partners. The senior partner in the hardwoods department was a rather crusty old man, who was driven
to the office every morning by a coachman with a four-wheeled
carriage. The office was very Dickensian. In the counting house
in the hardwoods department there was a long sloping mahogany desk, with seats on each side for three men facing each
other. The same men had sat in the same seats for about twenty
years. In between them was a brass ledge laden with thick,
heavy ledgers and account books, all bound in leather. Copies
of all documents and letters were printed into the books by
being pressed in large metal presses, which had to be screwed
down. Loose-leaf copies were not allowed and no female typists
were employed. The manager of this department was a rather
fearsome old character who always dressed in a black frock coat
and striped trousers. The other men had to wear dark suits,
though I think sports coats were permitted on Saturday mornings.

The offices occupied several floors and communication
between them was by speaking tube. One would blow down
the tube, which sounded a whistle at the other end, on the lower

floor; the recipient of the message would then have to remove the whistle and put his ear to the tube, when conversation could start. The juniors delighted to blow the whistle and then, when the hearer put his ear to the tube, instead of speaking they would blow again, very hard. It is incredible that such methods were still being followed in the 1920s.

After a year doing my office-boy chores, I was promoted to the shipping department, which was much more congenial. As agents for the owners, our firm had to make arrangements for the import of their goods into London. Some cargoes were discharged onto the dockyard quays, many others were discharged over the side into barges, for London lightermen had an immemorial right to receive cargoes into their barges without paying any charges. Barges had to be ordered and it was important that they should be in place when the cargoes were ready to be discharged, otherwise there would be demurrage charges to pay.

One of my new duties was to tour round the offices of the London shipping companies and go carefully through the ships' manifests to see if any goods destined for us were included in the cargo. Often I had to go with the bills of lading, to exchange them for delivery notes, so that our customers could collect the wood they had purchased from the docks. Frequently I had to go to the giant headquarters of the Port of London Authority on Tower Hill, to pay the port rates, and then to the Custom House in Lower Thames Street, to register the imports.

All this work meant that I had to be out for a large part of the day. Provided I got the work done, I was my own boss and could make the calls when I liked and as I liked. This job I found most enjoyable and I remained in it for the next five years.

My immediate boss was also out most of the day and no one knew quite where he was or what he was doing. He had a large circle of friends amongst the shipping offices, lighterage firms and port authorities and spent much time having refreshment with them. As he was an exceedingly kind man, much of his time was taken up with performing kind acts or making arrangements to help his friends, few of whom had any direct connection with our business.

One of his endearing characteristics was his habit of dealing with correspondence; he had evolved his own system, which consisted of having a large tin trunk, into which he put most of his letters and many other documents, all mixed up. About twice a year he would spend a day clearing out the trunk. As, by then, most of the enquiries had answered themselves, he managed to exist with remarkably little paperwork.

Through the many hours I spent outside, I developed a considerable love for the City of London. I became familiar not only with its streets, but with its many narrow little alleys and hidden courts, its quiet little closed churchyards, its old inns and the wharves and stairs by the river.

Nor did I confine my interest to the Square Mile of the City. By the Underground I could be at Charing Cross or St James's Park in a quarter of an hour. So I became a regular attender of Royal shows and processions, like the Opening of Parliament and the visits of foreign potentates, and I would sometimes eat a picnic lunch in the park.

But the aspect of City life which made the most profound impression on me was the churches. Not all the fifty-odd parish churches of the Elizabethan and Caroline periods were still in existence, but a considerable number remained until the 1940 blitz. At night time, of course, the City was almost completely deserted, but during the day some 500,000 people were coming into the City; in fact, most of their waking day was spent in the parishes of the City churches.

The value of the church sites was often enormous. Some people advocated pulling down the churches and selling the sites in order to build churches in outer suburbs. Fortunately this vandalism was strongly resisted. Although some of the churches seemed asleep, and were comparatively unused, many others had a full programme of lunchtime services, organ recitals and meetings, and their clergy seized to the full their opportunities for witness and evangelism.

I became a frequent attender at these lunchtime services. Sometimes I heard some of the most arresting preachers of the Church of England. Studdert-Kennedy (of Woodbine Willie fame) was rector of St Edmund, King and Martyr, at the end of our lane in Lombard Street. St Mary-le-Bow in Cheapside had a full programme, with often outstanding speakers, both clerical and lay. St Michael's, Cornhill, was famed for its music. But the church which came to mean most to me was All Hallows, Barking-by-the-Tower, next to the Tower of London.

The Archbishop of Canterbury, who was patron, had appointed as vicar the Reverend P B (Tubby) Clayton, largely in order that he would have a base for building up Toc H. He was away a great deal, but he managed to maintain a large staff of assistant priests. Some of these later became well known and joined the ranks of the episcopate, notably Cuthbert Bardsley, Tom Savage and Michael Coleman. The church was very lively and active. Unlike most of the City incumbents, who lived out in the suburbs, Tubby Clayton and his staff lived in the parish. As the years passed, he gradually established several residential hostels in the parish, three for men and two for women, so, in addition to the clergy, there was a resident community who provided a nucleus for the services and the many activities.

After a few years in the City, I was feeling very unsettled and insecure in my own religious life. My father had been a lifelong Nonconformist and my mother was an Anglican. As a boy I had attended both their churches, but I had never been confirmed. After one of the midday services at All Hallows, which was being conducted by the vicar, I went up to him very diffidently and said: 'Please can I be prepared for confirmation?'

'Good, good,' replied Tubby, 'but I am a wicked old man. I will introduce you to my curate, George Moore, and he will give you a good preparation.' So I met the priest who was to have a very great influence on my life.

George Moore was then about thirty-two years old. He was the son of a shopkeeper in Cranbrook, Kent. As a boy and young man, his two great enthusiasms were the organ and Scouting.

The Reverend P B ('Tubby') Clayton showing Queen Mary round All Hallows-by-the-Tower Church

While quite young he became a parish organist and later became a very gifted musician. With his brother, he helped to run the local troop of Scouts. As a countryman, he had extensive knowledge of natural history and country ways. He was very good at bird identification and, all his life, he was a very good axeman and knowledgeable about trees and wild flowers. Stars were another of his interests and he loved to share with youngsters his knowledge of the constellations. All these interests found a perfect outlet when he took boys away to camp.

He loved the life under canvas and was, in every way, an experienced camper. Camp cooking over a wood fire was one of his greatest specialities and, with his pleasant voice and musical background, the camp-fire singsongs he conducted remained as magical memories to all who took part in them. But the quality which made him such an outstanding leader was his capacity to win the loyalty and affection of youngsters and his deep understanding of their needs and potentialities.

When the war came in 1914, he left his Kentish village and enlisted in the county regiment, the Buffs. He was soon promoted from the ranks to be an NCO and, after some months spent training recruits, he was recommended for a commission.

As a young officer, he was sent out to join his regiment at the Battle of the Somme and later moved to the Ypres Salient. While he was there he went, on one occasion, to Talbot House, the soldiers' club (and much more) which had been established at Poperinge, a few miles behind the front line. This had been started by a chaplain, the Reverend P B Clayton, later the founder of the worldwide movement known as Toc H. This first encounter between Tubby and George Moore was the beginning of a lifelong friendship. After this, whenever his duties permitted, George Moore would return for a visit to Talbot House.

Later he was seconded to the Royal Engineers as a brigade gas officer and spent the rest of the war giving instruction in gas warfare. He came through the war without being wounded, having survived numerous dangerous situations, but his lungs were affected by contact with phosgene gas, which was undoubtedly the cause of the severe attacks of asthma from which he suffered for the rest of his life.

He could never understand why he had come through the war alive when so many of his friends and comrades had been killed. It was clear to him that his life was not his own; he must spend whatever health and life he had left in the work of training boys and men to fill the gaps left by those who had given their all for their country.

After the war he was accepted as an ordinand and went for training: first to Knutsford, the remarkable theological college established for service candidates in an ex-prison; then to Queen's College, Oxford, as an organ scholar. When he was ready for ordination, two men had a friendly confrontation to secure his services. Baden-Powell wanted him as an instructor for scoutmasters at his training centre at Gillwell Park and Tubby Clayton wanted him as curate at All Hallows. In the end, they reached a compromise: he was to join the staff at All Hallows, but was to be allowed two or three months a year to run training camps and other activities in the Scout movement.

This was the man who prepared me for confirmation. Week after week for some months I went to his flat on Tower Hill for an individual class and received a very full and comprehensive course of instruction. It was 'conversational Christianity'; teaching given informally, and with humour, while we sat in armchairs before a fire.

I was eventually confirmed in All Hallows church, by Bishop Edward Talbot, retired bishop of Winchester and father of Gilbert Talbot, after whom the first Talbot house had been named. Bishop Talbot came year after year; almost until his death, to take the All Hallows service. He was very old, lame and deaf when he confirmed me, but I have always felt it a great privilege that this fine old saint laid his hands on my head.

Before my confirmation I made my first confession. I found this a great ordeal but, before giving me absolution, Father Moore gave me most wise and inspiring counsel. I shall never

The Reverend Father George Moore

forget the deep sense of peace and joy which I experienced after my first confession.

Father Moore continued to be my confessor for many years and almost all of any good that there has been in my priesthood has been due to him and to his wise direction.

He used to hear confessions in the little crypt chapel of St Francis, in All Hallows church. This became a very precious and beloved shrine to me – and to many hundreds of other people. Before great festivals, Father Moore would spend several hours each day hearing confessions, as he had become known to an increasing number of penitents as a wise and holy Father-in-God.

Looking back over my life, I realise that one of its greatest blessings has been the practice of regular confession. After the death of Father Moore, and sometimes before that when he was not available, I made my confessions to other priests and have been privileged to be counselled by some outstandingly wise and sympathetic confessors.

Especially, I am grateful for the wonderful ministry of absolution exercised by the Cowley fathers at their London centre, St Edward's House. Many times I have gone there with a sad heart and left refreshed, inspired and encouraged.

Father Keble Talbot, and other members of the Community of the Resurrection, have also given me great help. Other outstanding confessors whose memory I shall always hold dear include Eric Abbott who, when dean of Westminster, was never too busy to minister to me, Father Eves of St Alban's, Holborn, Francis Underhill of the Grosvenor Chapel and the beloved Father Algy of the Franciscans.

I can never understand those Anglican clergymen who fail to give clear teaching concerning the availability of the Sacrament of Penance in the Church of England.

Nothing can be clearer than the Prayer Book teaching contained in the Exhortation in the Communion service:

And because it is requisite, that no man should come to the Holy Communion, but with a full trust in God's mercy, and with a quiet conscience; therefore if there be any of you, who by this means cannot quiet his own conscience herein, but requireth further comfort or counsel, let him come to me, or to some other discreet and learned Minister of God's word, and open his grief, that by the ministry of God's word he may receive the benefit of absolution, together with spiritual counsel and advice, to the quieting of his conscience, and avoiding of all scruple and doubtfulness.

I suppose some priests fail to give teaching about going to confession because they are scared of being thought too High Church, or do not want to face the criticism or disapproval of some of their parishioners. But, at the end of the road, it may rest heavily on their consciences that they have failed to exercise the commission laid upon them at their ordination, when the solemn words were said:

Receive the Holy Ghost for the office and work of a priest in the Church of God, now committed unto thee by the imposition of our hands. Whose sins thou dost forgive they are forgiven; and whose sins thou dost retain they are retained. And be thou a faithful dispenser of the Word of God and of His Holy Sacraments.

I have always thought of Father Moore as the Curé d'Ars of the Church of England. He served the Church as a priest for over fifty years, but he never received any preferment or Church honour.

Although he lived for nearly twenty years within half an hour of the West End, with all its theatres, concert halls and art galleries, he hardly ever went out of his City parish. For a number of years I do not think I ever saw him dressed in a lounge suit, as he lived almost always in a cassock, except when he was wearing khaki shirt and shorts during his weeks of camping.

I was reminded of him when I read von Hugel's memories of the Abbé Huvelin*, in his book *Eternal Life*:

* von Hugel, Baron Friedrich, *Eternal Life*, London, J M Dent, 1912.

... and finally, there is before my mind, with all the vividness resulting from direct personal intercourse and deep spiritual obligations, the figure of the Abbé Huvelin, who died only in 1910. A gentleman of birth and breeding ... this deep and heroic personality deliberately preferred to 'write in souls'; whilst occupying, during 35 years, a supernumerary unpaid post in a large Parisian parish. There, suffering from gout in the eyes and brain, and normally lying prone in a darkened room, he served souls with the supreme authority of self-oblivious love, and brought light and purity and peace to countless troubled sorrowing and sinful souls.

Father Moore was used by many people for spiritual advice and counselling. He had a great number of penitents, who came from a wide circle. He, like the Abbé Huvelin, preferred to 'write in souls'.

Through his teaching and example, I learned to revere some of the heroes of the Catholic revival in the Anglican Church, such as Father Lowder, who went to work in the docklands area of the East End of London in 1856 and died there in 1880. When he went there, of the 733 houses in the parish, 154 were brothels. Disease and vice were rampant. During his stay, the Church of St Peter's was built in the London docks, as well as schools for 600 children. When he began work there were barely half a dozen communicants in the district; when he died they numbered 500. The present Bishop of Chichester* wrote this about him recently:

Charles Lowder was a pioneer of the new school of parish priests, who restored the Eucharist to its central place in the Christian life and through the manner of the celebration brought a sense of light and love and joy to a people whose lives were stunted and dominated by evil. Naturally he encountered opposition. There were riots and, on two Sundays, the mob took possession of the choir stalls, pelted and defaced the altar hangings and

* An extract from a sermon preached on 30 October 1991, printed in the December 1991 issue of the Chichester leaflet and reprinted by kind permission of Dr Eric Kemp, the Right Reverend Bishop of Chichester.

threw down the cross. Lowder's life was in danger and he had to be protected by members of the congregation against a mob that tried to throw him into the docks. Ostensibly these attacks were on principles of religion. In fact they were financed by those whose living was made out of the vices of the district.

... the year of the riots was followed by the dreadful cholera epidemic. It became necessary to set up temporary hospitals and of this work Lowder took charge helped by friends and nursing sisters. From the first he had established a daily Eucharist and there he and his helpers gathered at the altar every morning before going out to the dreadful and dangerous labour of the day. One who later worked in the parish said; 'The poor people have never forgotten the lesson they learned during that fearful time.'

The children flocked round Lowder, sheltering under his cloak, and it is said that, from that time, priests began to be called 'Father'.

Later in the century there was Father Stanton who, for nearly fifty years, served as an unbeneficed curate at St Alban's, Holborn. The great theologian Bishop Charles Gore*, founder of the Community of the Resurrection, wrote of him: 'It was Father Stanton of St Alban's, Holborn, who taught me to make my confession, to love the Mass and to fast on Fridays.'

Although one of the outstanding preachers of his generation, Father Stanton never received any honours or preferment from the Church of England. Towards the end of his ministry there was a meeting of 750 men in Holborn Town Hall, to present him with a testimonial which had the signatures of about 4,000 men. During his speech in reply, Father Stanton said:

Why are you here like this? To do me this honour and to show your love for me? It is because God has given me something better than emolument and far better than position. God has given to me, blessed by His Holy Name, the love of my fellow men.

* Bishop Charles Gore (1853–1932), quoted in Prestige, L, *Life of Charles Gore*, London, Heinemann, 1938.

After he died, in March 1913, the London traffic was halted and crowds lined the streets as his coffin was borne from St Alban's to Waterloo station, on its way to the parish burial ground at Woking.

The week after his death, *Truth* printed these lines by R M Freeman. They may not be great poetry, but they expressed what many hundreds of people thought:

> Goodbye, Father.
> We didn't all agree with you,
> Nor eye to eye could see with you
> In all you held and said.
> But we saw the single mind of you,
> The zeal and faith combined of you,
> And the shining light you shed.
>
> Goodbye, Father.
> For place, ambitions, fighters strive,
> Her priests for stalls and mitres strive
> Make gain of serving God.
> You chose the poor, the lowly road,
> Renunciation's holy road
> That the Man of Sorrows trod.
>
> Goodbye, Father.
> Some called you Romish, what of that?
> Who knew you reckoned not of that
> On deeds, not names, they leant.
> From Nazareth comes any good?
> Thence came one doing many good
> And in His steps you went.
>
> Goodbye, Father.
> So passing, saintly, through the world
> You brought His message to the world
> In the only way it heeds.
> Not those who make a strife of Christ

But those who live the life of Christ
Can give it what it needs.

Another greatly loved priest of the Catholic revival was Father
Dolling who, at about this time, was exercising his ministry in
the dockyard slums of St Agatha's Portsmouth, labouring
amongst the sailors and dockers, the drunks and the prostitutes
who at this time lived in this very overcrowded and run-down
district. Conrad Noel* wrote these memories of him:

> I went to Father Dolling in the Portsmouth slums, and the com-
> panionship of this radical priest gave me an insight into pastoral
> work which I could not otherwise have gained. It should be an
> everyday thing for a parish priest to be rung up like a doctor,
> night and day, and Father Dolling was always on call. Sometimes,
> at midnight or at three a.m., he would be called for to administer
> the last rites of the Church, or to settle a dispute amongst neigh-
> bours, and hurriedly throwing a cassock over his night things he
> would set out and not return for hours.
>   . . . St Agatha's, Landport, was the Winchester College Mission.
> It was then a temporary church, but always crowded on Sundays
> with worshippers, largely of the down-and-out variety. Dolling
> was not a great preacher, but his simplicity and directness
> touched the hearts of his congregation and, as he passed up the
> aisle in a gorgeous cope in the procession, he would bless
> the people and lay his hand on the heads of those near him.

Eventually Dolling was driven out of his parish by the then
Bishop of Winchester, who objected to the altar in the Chapel of
All Souls, which the father had erected and where he said
Requiem Masses for the souls of the faithful departed, many of
whom had been drowned at sea.

Only a few years later, the same service was being said in St
Paul's Cathedral for Lord Kitchener.

In many ways Father George Moore was a true follower and
successor of these heroes of the Catholic revival, although All

* Quoted in *Autobiography*, Conrad Noel, edited with an introduction by Sidney
  Dark, London, J M Dent and Sons, 1949.

Hallows was not, in any sense, in the mainstream of Anglo-Catholicism. The services were conducted in strict accordance with the Prayer Book and although, at the Sung Eucharist, vestments were worn and servers arrayed in albs, incense was not used and there were none of the outward trimmings of Roman ceremonial.

All Hallows parish, in the City, would not have been thought of as very propitious soil for a pastoral ministry among young people. When I first knew it, apart from 'outsiders' resident in the Toc H hostels, there were only about four or five families who lived in the parish.

I became very friendly with one of these families. The father was caretaker of an old building used by a firm of wine importers. It was approached through an archway leading off Great Tower Street. Unseen from the street and hidden behind a modern block of offices, it was a very interesting house indeed, containing some rooms with fine panelling. It had been, at one time in past centuries, the Spanish Embassy. The caretaker's flat was on the top floor. I used to love to drop in about teatime, when the wife would be bathing her baby in a tin bath in front of an open fire.

It was startling, yet comforting, to find such a domestic scene in the midst of modern commercial life, with offices all round buzzing with telephones and typewriters and all the frantic activities of the financial heart of the City. Alas, this fine historic old house was burned down in the London fire blitz.

The mother of the family was a remarkable woman. Of her four children (the only children who lived in the parish), one later became ordained and retired as an archdeacon after a distinguished career; one son was given a commission in the war and later became an outstanding governor in the prison service; the daughter became a nurse, until she was married; and the baby grew up to fill an important post in the Bank of England. All four began their education at a nearby elementary school and I think they would be the first to bear witness to the important influence on their lives of Father Moore, who not only taught them their religion, but also shared with them his love for classical music and books and civilised living.

Although so few youngsters lived in the parish, youngsters from surrounding districts came in, often attracted by the All Hallows Guide company and the first City of London Scout troop, which rejoiced in the title of 'The Lord Mayor's Own'. During the twenty years of Father Moore's ministry at All Hallows, eight boys from the Scout troop were accepted for ordination. Several girls from the Guide company found their vocation in the religious life, joining the Community of St Mary at Wantage and some other orders; others became nurses.

Perhaps, at one period, the influence of the good father was almost too strong; it looked for a while as though these were the only vocations about which he was enthusiastic. However, love will find a way and, over the years, there were a number of romances amongst the youngsters of this very happy parish family. One of the greatest joys of my life has been to keep in touch, ever since, with some of these couples and their children.

During his ministry probably more than a score of men from a wider circle of acquaintance found their vocation to Holy Orders through his example and teaching.

Father Moore would, I think, have given his assent to the old adage: 'The effective man is the selective man.' I remember him saying:

> Each one of us has only a limited amount of jam to spread. Either he takes a large number of pieces of bread and butter; in this case the jam will be spread very thin. Or else he is content to take a few slices; in this case the jam will be spread very thick.

In 1940 Father Moore, who had been very ill with asthma, went to Switzerland for treatment by Dr Rollier. He was marooned in the neutral country once the war had really started. After his health improved, he was able to exercise a remarkable ministry at the English church at Berne. The congregation there had been greatly increased by large numbers of RAF pilots and escaped prisoners-of-war who had managed to cross the frontiers into

Switzerland. Here, again, he was able to use his old skills of giving organ recitals, conducting singsongs and exercising a pastoral ministry based on friendship.

When the war was over, he returned to England, to find that All Hallows church had been destroyed in the bombing and not yet rebuilt; moreover, the unique spiritual family which had been built up on Tower Hill was scattered far and wide. Things could never be the same again and Father Moore found it very difficult to find the right niche. Although many friends who admired his work tried to help with suggestions, he was a difficult man to place.

After some time, he was appointed chaplain of St Helen's and St Katherine's School at Abingdon, which was run by the Wantage sisters. There was a fine chapel and he collected money for a splendid new organ. He lived in the chaplain's house and his way of life carried on much as before. After some years, as he and the sisters did not see eye to eye about some aspects of the girls' training, he left.

Then he accepted a curacy at St Michael's Church, Oxford. Although the churchmanship there was on rather different lines from his own, one advantage of this appointment was that he was given, as his home, a very pleasant old stone house. This became his base for some years. Usually he had several undergraduates as his lodgers and, from his home, he was able to exercise much the same kind of ministry as before, with a large circle of penitents and people coming for individual counsel or instruction.

After a few years, he was left a small legacy and bought a little terraced house at New Hinksey, Oxford. By then, he was very deaf and often ill with asthma. He became a well-known figure in Oxford, as he pottered about in his cassock and cloak, shopping or visiting friends, and he became an honorary priest at St Mary Magdalene's, Oxford, which he loved deeply.

I am thankful to remember that, when he was in his eighties, I drove him in my car to Montreux, to visit old friends. He was then a very frail old man and he died in 1976. Like his hero, Father Stanton, he had served the Church for over fifty years as an unbeneficed priest and he, too, was given the love of his fellow men.

It was 1927 when I was confirmed and I was twenty-one years old. After my confirmation I became more closely connected with All Hallows. I became a server and sometimes served the vicar, Reverend P B Clayton, at a midweek celebration. This meant leaving my home in the suburbs at 6.30 am, to be ready for the service at All Hallows at 8 am.

Tubby was a short little man, built, as he himself said, like a human gasometer. He had a rather fine deep voice and used to greet people with a friendly smile, blinking at them from behind big spectacles. He took very little care over his appearance and often dressed in a blue blazer with somewhat dishevelled grey trousers.

Food did not interest him very much; he would be unaware whether he was eating an exquisite meal at an expensive restaurant or bangers-and-mash at a roadside cafe. But he valued mealtimes as a useful opportunity for meeting people and thought that hospitality was a very important part of the Christian life. There were always several guests at the vicarage dining table and sometimes, to the despair of his housekeeper, he would, at the last moment, invite another four guests to a meal.

After I had served for him at a midweek Eucharist, he would often invite me back to breakfast. We would walk from the church round Trinity Square to the large house which served as parish offices, Toc H lunch club and vicarage. Usually, in those days, there would be, standing by the kerbside, large vans and carts hauled by splendid shire horses. Tubby always had lumps of sugar in his cassock pocket, which he doled out to the horses on our way back to breakfast. One never knew whom one would meet at the breakfast table. I remember one occasion when I sat next to a recently-retired governor-general of Australia; on my other side was the local postman, who had just called to deliver the mail and had been asked by the vicar to sit down for a cup of tea.

Through his work for Toc H, Tubby had often met and entertained members of the Royal Family and was a friend of many well-known and influential people. He was also very good at extracting money from rich men, in order to further the good causes in which he was engaged. One very wealthy supporter was Lord Wakefield, the oil millionaire. His generous support made possible many projects in which Tubby was involved. Tubby once said that when he died they should carve on his tombstone the words from St Luke's gospel 'the beggar died . . .'

Perhaps the most memorable project which Tubby inspired, and which Lord Wakefield eventually financed, was the restoration of Tower Hill. When I first knew Tower Hill, to the east of All Hallows church and completely dominating the approach to the entrance of the Tower of London, there was a huge ugly brick warehouse owned by the Mazawattee Tea Company. This was the first thing that visitors to London saw as they approached the Tower. For years Tubby had badgered, unsuccessfully, the City Corporation to remove this eyesore from what was one of the finest historical sites in England. Eventually, with Lord Wakefield's help, he raised enough money to purchase the site, demolish the monstrous building and create in its place a delightful garden, which was open to the public.

But, although Tubby had many influential friends, he never lost touch with the common man and had a prodigious memory for people he had known and helped, perhaps many years before. He had a succession of ADCs, usually young undergraduates who had a year to spare before going on to a theological college or to some other work. Their task was to be a kind of secretary cum valet cum companion; to buy rail or air tickets, to look up timetables and to try to ensure that the vicar arrived at the right destination not too dreadfully late.

Tubby kept in his study a number of loose-leaf address books, arranged geographically, containing hundreds of names and addresses. Whenever he went on his numerous journeys through the country, Tubby would sit in the car, consulting the appropriate address book, and would instruct his ADC where and when he wished to look up an old friend. This was doubtless the reason he often arrived very late for appointments.

Years later, when he visited me while I was working in Portsmouth, I had to conduct him to a big meeting which he was addressing in the city. But, on the way, he kept on remembering the little terraced homes which had been lived in by boys in his Bible class thirty years before. We had to stop frequently, to see if they were still there, and arrived at the meeting very late indeed.

He was often quite unpredictable and I remember one example of this. All Hallows had two faithful supporters, middle-aged spinsters who lived in a comfortable home at Chislehurst, though they drove up to services at All Hallows. On one occasion, Tubby rang them one Sunday morning.

'Dear Sophie,' he said, 'I have a man here whom I am trying to help but who has threatened to commit suicide. I think it might have a calming effect on him if he was brought into a friendly Christian home for a visit. So please may I bring him down to tea? We should get to you about 4 pm.'

The two somewhat prim spinsters agreed to this suggestion and at once issued orders to their cook and parlourmaid to prepare the necessary buttered scones and toast and cakes. At about 5 pm a large car drew up outside their house. Out of it stepped the Reverend Tubby and five other men. The sisters sent urgent orders to the kitchen for extra supplies and the tea party went on merrily in the drawing-room. All the time the sisters were looking at each other and wondering which of their visitors was the potential suicide.

About half past six, Tubby and his companions thanked their hostesses for a delightful tea and stood up to leave. As they were getting into the car, Sophie whispered to Tubby: 'Dear Father, do tell us, which was the man who had threatened to commit suicide?'

Tubby paused for a moment, then said: 'Oh, him. In the end we decided not to bring him and he stayed at home.'

Tubby drove himself very hard and fortunately he was very

strong physically. For years he had a night shorthand-typist as well as a day secretary. He would sit up night after night, dictating letters till well after midnight. On occasion he would work all through the night, then have a bath, go across to church for the early celebration and carry on all day as usual.

One of the reasons why Tubby made contact with so many different types of men, and helped them to find Christian faith, was that he enabled them to feel needed and that they had some contribution to make. After he had met someone for the first time, Tubby would say: 'I wonder what we can ask him to do.' He often referred to the story in the Gospels concerning Zacheus. This pompous little man had so wanted to see Jesus, of whom he had heard so much, that he climbed up into a tree to see Him pass. Our Lord looked up and saw him too and realised something of the longing in his heart: 'Zacheus, be quick and come down, for I must stay at your house today.'

Tubby always had work for men to do, 'They that do the will shall know of the doctrine.' He felt that too often when the Church approached men it asked what it could do to help them, but Tubby approached the matter from the opposite angle: 'Give a man work to do and he may find his soul not hitherto discovered ... let the Church make it clear to men that it has genuine work for them to do, not only pews for them to occupy.'

'Religion', he wrote*, 'is in men waiting to be brought out ... It was a habit with Our Lord to anticipate a kindly nature in man, and thus to prompt the proof of it.'

There is no doubt that, between the wars, Tubby Clayton exercised a remarkable ministry. Few priests have helped more men to seek ordination. All Hallows church became a strong centre of worship and activity.

I remember the annual Corporate Communion for London members of Toc H on Ascension Day each year. Held at 7 am on a working day, it was attended by a congregation of over 500 men. After the service and outdoor procession on Tower

* Quoted by Kenneth Prideaux-Brune in his memoir of Tubby, *A Living Witness*, Aylesbury, Toc H, 1983.

Hill, all the nearby branches of Lyons and ABC tea shops were full of office workers, breakfasting together before setting off for their daily work.

A number of residential hostels (or 'marks') were established in London and other big cities for young men who had to work and live away from home.

One special need which had evoked Tubby's concern was the work amongst lepers overseas, especially in countries of the British Commonwealth. A considerable number of men, influenced by Tubby's advocacy, gave several years of their lives to work overseas in leper clinics and homes.

It is undoubtedly true that after the Second World War the influence of Toc H waned and its membership became more elderly. Times had changed and the movement did not appeal, on the whole, to the younger generation. It had, perhaps, become rather backward-looking, with its idealism deriving from the comradeship of Poperinge in 1915. Much of its ethos had centred round the personality of Philip Clayton and as, inevitably with the passing of the years, he lost some of his old drive, the momentum of Toc H slowed down, though some branches were still doing useful work in the community.

When Tubby died in December 1972, aged eighty-seven, St Paul's Cathedral was crammed to the doors, mainly by men, for his Memorial Service. So many men, and I was one of them, wished to give thanks for a holy and humble servant of God.

In my confirmation classes I had been encouraged to take up some kind of Christian work and not just spend my spare time enjoying myself. I joined the Tower Hill branch of Toc H. In the initiation ceremony the following dialogue takes place, as the candidate is admitted by the branch chairman before the Lamp of Remembrance which every branch holds in memory of the Elder Brethren of Toc H who had given their lives in the war:

'What first lit this lamp?'
'Unselfish sacrifice.'
'What alone will maintain it?'
'Unselfish service.'

'What is service?'

'The rent we pay for our room on earth.'

As part of my rent, I was sent by the branch to help at a boys' club which was run by the parish of Holy Trinity, Hoxton. So on one or two nights a week, after I had finished at the office and had some tea, I would take a bus to Shepherdess Walk, Hoxton. In those days Hoxton was a very rough area. The club consisted of one or two rooms in a rather dilapidated parish building, in which there were a billiards table, facilities for table tennis and a canteen.

After I had been going for some weeks, I noticed that some of the boys whose faces had become familiar seemed to have disappeared. When I asked after them, I was told they were away on holiday. It seemed to me rather strange that boys from such a poor district would go away on holiday but then it dawned on me that this was a euphemism to explain their absence; in fact, they had been sent to a prison or reformatory.

One night, when I was the only adult in charge of the club, the boys seemed very restless. Suddenly one of them produced an airgun and popped off, one by one, all the electric light bulbs in the club. In the darkness and mayhem which followed, considerable damage was done to the club premises.

Not long afterwards the vicar of the parish, Father Ford, a tall figure in cassock and biretta, came into the club. I gathered he took a rather dim view of my ability as a club leader. But by this time I had come to see that the boys needed more than someone to teach them to play billiards or table tennis. They had deeper needs and, gradually, the challenge came to me to consider the possibility that I was being called to serve God as an ordained minister.

Later that summer my parents had their annual summer holiday at Swanage. I went with them and it was the last time in my life that we had a family holiday. My father drove us down in his old Morris Cowley and I sat in the dickey at the back. I remember clearly that drive on a lovely July day. The cottage gardens of Hampshire and Dorset were ablaze with roses in their summer glory. All the way I was debating in my mind the question of what I was going to do with my life.

At that time I was very fond of a girl at home but in those days there were no State grants for higher education and the Church had few grants to offer to ordination candidates of limited means. It was clear to me that, if I offered myself for ordination, I would have to pay for my training largely through my own savings – and would have to put aside any thoughts of romance. I had to decide: either to carry on with the romance or else to go forward with ordination training. I could not do both.

My mind was in such turmoil that, before our holiday at Swanage was over, I felt I must talk things out with Father Moore. At that time he was camping with the All Hallows Scouts at Lepe, in Hampshire. I left Swanage by train and got out at Beaulieu Road station, on an exceedingly hot and very lovely July day. From the station, it was an eight-mile walk through the village of Beaulieu to Lepe, a little hamlet on the shores of the Solent. I was wearing a well-cut blazer with immaculate grey flannel trousers.

When I eventually arrived at the campsite, I was persuaded to stay the night and, as I had not brought any luggage, I was loaned a sleeping-bag and khaki shirt and shorts. That evening, after Compline in the chapel tent, I walked with Father Moore from the meadow to Lepe beach. It was a perfect summer's night, with a full moon throwing a shaft of light over the sea and with the lights of Cowes twinkling across the Solent. We sat on the shore for an hour or so and talked and as a result I came to what, for me, was a very big decision.

Next day I returned to London. I gave a month's notice of resignation from my job at the timber brokers and, at the end of September, I was entered as a student in the Faculty of Theology at King's College, London.

As my academic qualifications were so meagre, I joined the preliminary year so that my general studies could be brought up to approximately matriculation levels. After this I spent three years in the course for the theological diploma of the Associate-ship of King's College, which was accepted as an alternative to the General Ordination Examination.

The Theological Faculty consisted of about 150 men, who were part of a college of 2,000 undergraduates. There were large faculties for art, sciences, engineering and medicine. Theological students were encouraged to play a full part in the under-graduate activities of the college and, in my third year, I became the junior vice-president of the Union Society.

There were some hilarious moments during my time of train-ing at King's and I suppose I am one of the few people who have been chased by an elephant in the streets of the City of London.

Each year the Lord Mayor's Show, on its return from the Law Courts to the Mansion House, passes along the Thames Embankment. The students at King's had long had a tradition of bringing their college mascot to the Embankment entrance of the college in order to make obeisance to the Lord Mayor as he passed. The college mascot was a life-sized lion made of red plaster, which had been acquired from the plinth of the Red Lion brewery. One year I had the task of being one of the team of four who bore on their shoulders the stretcher on which the lion stood.

It happened that year that the Lord Mayor had had business connections with India and included in his procession a large Indian elephant, with bearer in Indian dress and turban. When the elephant saw our lion, which he assumed was alive, he stopped the procession and, lifting his head, gave out a loud roar. Then, with heavy deliberate steps, he made straight for us. We at once dropped the lion on the ground and fled for our lives. When the elephant reached the lion, he turned it over with his foot, sniffed it and kicked it away in disgust. This had caused a stampede amongst the crowds lining the route and mounted police galloped up bravely to restore order. It was the first time in living memory that the Lord Mayor's show had been disrupted. The London papers were full of the incident and we received a severe wigging from the college principal although, as we said in mitigation, we could not have anticipated this happening.

It was an odd place to prepare for Holy Orders, but the staff in the theological faculty included some outstanding scholars. The dean when I began there was Dr W R Matthews, later dean of St Paul's. Other members of the teaching staff included Professor E J Bicknell, Professor Claud Jenkins (the Church historian), Professor Relton and Professor Richard Hanson (who later became dean and who was an authority on Thomas Aquinas). Towards the end of my time Eric Abbott was appointed chaplain. Even then, he was showing the charm and ability which was later to make him one of the most renowned and loved deans of Westminster Abbey.

It was a brilliant staff and, no doubt, the contact which ordinands had with their contemporaries in other faculties was not without its value. But, as two-thirds of its members were not yet residential, the theological faculty lacked the disciplined training in the devotional life which was given in smaller theological colleges, where the men shared a corporate life.

The Strand was an odd place to begin preparation for the ministry. After lectures in the mornings, some of the men used to slip off to matinées in West End theatres. On the other hand, they had opportunities to hear some of the best preachers of the day in London's churches.

We were encouraged to play a full part in the sporting life of the college. I became captain of the faculty's soccer eleven, not because I had any skill at the game, but because the captain had to undertake all the secretarial chores and no one else wanted the job. We played fierce inter-denominational battles against Regent's Park Baptist College, Richmond Methodist College and St John's, Highbury, the evangelical college. But our greatest moment of glory came when we beat the Engineers in the final of King's Inter-Faculty Cup. I paid dearly for taking part in these soccer games for, in my last year, I had a painful collision on the pitch which caused serious damage to the lumbar vertebrae of my spine and eventually caused me a great deal of pain and trouble.

For two years I lived at home and travelled up to King's every day. My third year I spent at the Theological Hostel in Vincent Square, Westminster, which gave excellent opportunities for corporate life and worship. For the fourth year, I moved to a bed sitting-room at 16 Tower Hill, the home of Father Moore, a delightful little building which, sadly, was blown up during the war bombing. The house was built against a remaining part of the original Roman wall of the City. One wall of Father Moore's study was actually part of the Roman wall. My little room on the top floor had a superb view right over the Tower of London: the only medieval fortress in Europe which has been in continuous military occupation for nine hundred years.

During this year, I spent far too much time running the Rover crew of the All Hallows Scout troop and becoming involved in other ways with the life of All Hallows. But I have never regretted this year spent living in the City of London and joining in the vibrant life of the delightful spiritual family whose loyalties were centred on All Hallows.

At the end of these four years, I realised I badly needed to quieten down and be trained in the devotional life required of a priest. The College of the Resurrection at Mirfield most kindly allowed me to be attached to the college for four months. So I spent the time between September and December sharing in the disciplined life of the college and joining in the inspiring worship of the Community church.

Tubby Clayton had offered me a title at All Hallows church. I was thrilled about this, as I loved the parish very much and would have felt it a very great honour and privilege to begin my ministry there. But when my tutor at King's, Prebendary Bicknell, heard of this, he was horrified. He told me that, as All Hallows was not in any sense a normal parish, and as its vicar was away from his parish most of the time, I would not receive any training in the work of an ordinary Church of England parish. Instead, he advised me strongly to accept a curacy under the Reverend F E Croyden, rector of Chingford, who would carefully supervise my year as a deacon. I saw that this was wise advice, so I withdrew, sadly, my acceptance of the title at All Hallows and began my ministry, in December 1933, as curate of Chingford parish church, Essex.

During the four years of my preparation for ordination, there was one subject about which I knew I had to come to a decision. I believed that I had been called to be a priest, but I did not know what kind of priest I should be: was I to be a celibate priest or a married clergyman?

The thirty-second Article of the Church of England says:

Bishops priests and deacons are not commanded by God's law, either to vow the estate of single life or to abstain from marriage; therefore it is lawful for them, as for all other Christian men, to marry at their own discretion, as they shall judge the same to serve better to godliness.

Our Lord Jesus Christ gave up for Himself the right to have a wife and children; in order to accomplish His mission He had to be free from the restrictions and ties of family life. He said in Mark 10:19–30:

There is no man that hath left house, or brethren, or sisters, or father, or mother, or wife, or children for my sake and the gospel's, but he shall receive an hundredfold now in this time, houses and brethren, and sisters, and mothers, and children, and lands, with persecutions; and in the world to come eternal life.

It is interesting to note that Christ assured those who would give up marriage, for His sake and the gospel's, not only the reward of everlasting life but also the promise of receiving an hundredfold now in this life. Certainly His words have come true in many lives. We can think of the many nuns to whom the words of the psalmist could be applied: 'He hath made the barren woman to keep house; and to be a joyful mother of children.' We can also remember all those celibate priests who have been given a large family of spiritual children.

Both St Peter, who was married, and St Paul, who gave up

marriage for Christ's sake, have been honoured down the ages as the great Founder-Apostles of the Church. In the seventh chapter of his first letter to the Corinthians, Paul gave uncompromising teaching on the subject, although it is probable that his views were coloured by his belief that the end of the world was not far off. He said:

> ... He that is unmarried careth for the things that belong to the Lord, how he may please the Lord.
> But he that is married careth for the things that are of the world, how he may please his wife.

The Roman Catholic Church has enjoined, since the twelfth century, celibacy for the clergy. In the Eastern Orthodox Church priests are not marriageable: if they wish to marry, they may do so before ordination, but not afterwards; bishops are always appointed from the ranks of the celibate clergy. In the Church of England the compulsory celibacy of clergy was abolished in 1549.

I am very glad that our Church gives its ordinands the freedom to choose whether or not to marry, but I am very sure that the life and witness of the Anglican Church would be immensely strengthened if we had a higher proportion of celibate priests and bishops.

I would pay a warm tribute to the many splendid partnerships in clerical marriages. There are many married parsons who, with their wives, have made their vicarage open-house to the parish and have given cheer, hospitality and friendship to many lonely and sad folk. I admire, especially, those heroic wives of missionary priests who have gone with them to lonely outposts on the frontiers of the Church's worldwide mission. Some have weaned their babies far from medical help or the companionship of other white women. Also, without doubt, our country has gained through the lives of men and women born and reared in parsonage homes who have gone out to serve in Church and State.

But there is another side to the story. In some cases the harm done to the parish by the parson's wife has outweighed any good done by the incumbent. More often, the wife has become so discontented that she has nagged her husband until he has found another job. We all know cases where a man has been doing splendid work in difficult or uncongenial surroundings and has had to give it up because his wife has coveted a house or a district in a more pleasant environment.

I admire very much some of the younger wives who, in the changed conditions of modern life, have had to go out to work in order to supplement the family income. They try bravely to tackle the insoluble problem of holding down a job while running a home and endeavouring to be the vicar's wife. Not surprisingly, they often crack under the strain. There has been a sad increase in the number of broken clerical marriages.

Nor is the episcopal bench without its problems. Some bishops have been blessed with wives who have given them quiet and loyal support. But others of our present liberal establishment give the impression of being very hen-pecked.

The twentieth century has not been without its Mrs Proudies. In the past, episcopal nepotism has been a sad blot on the life of the Church. It is astounding how frequently, especially in the eighteenth and nineteenth centuries, married prelates gave lucrative preferment to their sons, sons-in-law and nephews.

But it has always seemed to me that the greatest drawback to a married ministry is that, often, married clergymen have contrived to make Christianity such a boring and bourgeois way of life. It might be thought impossible to make the Christian life boring, but some parsons and their wives seem to have settled down into a mediocre life of dull domestic respectability.

It became clear to me that I agreed with von Hugel*, when he wrote in his *Essays and Addresses*:

Certainly I know beyond the possibility of doubt that I myself could never have been regained by any but a celibate priest to

* von Hugel, *Essays and Addresses*, Dent, 1926.

purity and to God – however much, since I was thus costingly regained, I may appreciate the beneficence of a married clergy, and however clearly I perceive the dangers and drawbacks of too large an extension of obligatory celibacy.

I am sure that Almighty God does give to some men grace and strength to combine the vocations of Holy Orders and Holy Matrimony. But, for me, it had to be one or the other. Either I would get married and try to earn as much as possible to support my wife and children, or else I would seek ordination and give up thoughts of marriage.

Without doubt, I have been a very bad priest. But I have never regretted the decision I made at the age of twenty-seven: to remain celibate whatever the difficulties and problems. Unless I had opted for this pattern of the ministry, I would not have been ordained and I would have missed so much of absorbing work, friendship, affection and fulfilment of life.

8
Essex
1906–1922

> . . . look unto the rock whence ye are hewn,
> and to the hole of the pit whence ye are digged
> Isaiah 51.1

I was born in 1906, so I lived for four years in the Edwardian era. Our home was at Leytonstone in Essex, although later my parents moved further out – to Loughton. My father was a London businessman with an office in the City, in Finsbury Pavement. He worked on his own, as the London representative of a Birmingham firm of brass founders. He had been born and brought up in Sunderland.

His father was a sea captain, who owned his sailing schooner. In those days men would own their own ships and seek for cargo to be transported anywhere in the world. My grandfather was drowned at sea when his ship foundered in the China seas, with the loss of all hands.

After this blow to the family fortunes, my father, then a young man, came down to London to earn his living. He had to support his mother and two sisters, so there was little money to spare and he had to delay his own marriage.

He met my mother at her home at Tottenham; their marriage was blessed with three sons, of whom I was the youngest. I had the inestimable blessing of growing up in a very happy family. My parents were devoted to each other. They hated being apart and I never heard a cross word between them. They were very keen tennis players and one of my earliest memories is of being left in my pram in the sunshine by the side of a tennis court at their club.

I remember my first day at school, as I took an instant dislike to the idea and kicked my headmistress in the stomach as hard as I could. Gradually I settled down, but I never learned to love my schools.

Those were the days when middle-class families had a fortnight by the sea each summer. This was eagerly anticipated and caused great excitement. A large tin trunk would be filled with clothes and sent off by train labelled 'luggage in advance'. We would set off for the station by horse-cab and have another cab from Liverpool Street to London Bridge station.

My father was very fond of Deal, in Thanet, and we went there summer after summer for many years. In those days there were still a number of luggers hauled up on the beach. They were survivors from the times when they would ferry out pilots and mail and supplies to the many sailing vessels which would be anchored in the Channel off Deal waiting for a favourable wind. There were still a number of old salts who seemed to spend all day smoking and sitting by their boats. My father would encourage them to speak of rescues they had made in their luggers of sailors shipwrecked on the Goodwin Sands.

He loved the atmosphere of this ancient seaport town and, as I grew older, I learned to love it, too, especially the long walks past Deal and Walmer castles to Kingsdown, where the white cliffs of Dover began and one could ramble for miles on close-cropped springy turf.

We were staying there when war broke out, in August 1914. From their marine base, the Royal Marines marched off, with colours flying and the band playing, to entrain. I ran along beside the band. They went to defend Antwerp, but the city fell in a few days and the men spent the next four years in prisoner-of-war camps in Germany.

I have blurred memories of the war years. During the Zeppelin raids on London we spent many nights down in the cellar of our home, which my father had strengthened and fitted up as a shelter.

A German airship was shot down at Cuffley and I watched it sink in flames. I remember, also, going to see a nearby terrace of little homes which had been shattered and demolished by the heavy Zeppelin bombs; I saw then the kind of sights which were to become all too familiar twenty-five years later.

My oldest brother was aged fifteen at the outbreak of war and had just started work at an office in the City. I remember him coming home in 1915 and announcing to my father that he had joined the army. He had given his age falsely, as eighteen, and had been accepted by the London Rifle Brigade. My father was most concerned and went up next day to secure his release. The colonel saw him and persuaded my father that, as the boy was so keen, it would be best to let him remain in the LRB, but as a bugle-boy aged fifteen and not as a combatant. So he joined up but did not go overseas until he was turned eighteen, when he was wounded in Flanders.

I had been entered for Forest School, a minor public school near my home. But when war came my parents could not afford the fees and I went, instead, to the local high school. Most of the good masters were away in the army and the standard of teaching was very low. I became very lazy, lost all interest in school and got mixed up with the wrong set.

One summer during the war my parents had a holiday at Burnham-on-Crouch. While we were there a young man from the local parish, which was extremely Low Church, tried to influence me. I was repelled by his approaches and reacted so strongly against his efforts that, for a time, I was put off religion altogether. It is curious that, in the sixty years since I was ordained, I have scarcely ever had any contact with the extreme Low Church wing of the Church of England.

Our church has certainly developed in rigidly separate compartments. The extreme Protestant party has become almost a church within a church. They have their own party organisations, their own newspapers and magazines, their own boarding schools (firmly controlled so as to retain the same ethos), their own theological colleges to train evangelical clergy, their own missionary societies (which only employ workers of the same 'colour') and, worst of all, their own patronage trusts which, in the bad old days, bought up livings so that they could fill parishes with Low Church clergymen, irrespective of the needs or desires of the unfortunate parishioners. Fortunately, in recent years many of the younger generation of evangelicals have broken out of the narrow bounds which confined them and shed many of the old prejudices.

My mother was an Anglican, but my father was a Nonconformist. I grew up in a home where both my parents took their children with them to divine worship every Sunday.

My father attended a Baptist chapel, Fillebrook, which was very well known in that denomination and drew large congregations. The minister, in my boyhood days, was the Reverend John Macbeth; he was a fine character and a most eloquent and inspiring preacher. This was the era of family worship; Sunday by Sunday the same families would occupy the same pews, for which they paid a rent, father and mother and children sitting and worshipping together.

It is curious that, in the country areas in which I have lived in recent years, Nonconformity seems almost to have ceased to exist and many country chapels have been closed and sold. Perhaps they are paying the penalty for the very close links which used to exist between them and the Liberal party, for in my lifetime the Liberal party has changed from a position of great strength to one of almost insignificance in national life.

Ours was a fairly strict home. Alcohol was not drunk, except for a little wine at Christmas time. When I first went out to work, my father asked me to promise that I would not drink alcohol until I came of age. I kept the promise, but on my twenty-first birthday I went, with a group of fellow clerks from my office, to the nearest pub.

My parents were also strict sabbatarians and there were no Sunday games or outings and no Sunday newspapers. But it was a very happy home. My parents had many friends and loved entertaining, their special delight being in holding whist drives in our home.

I cannot remember my father ever talking to me about religion, but one memory is printed indelibly in my mind. We

had a houseful of visitors and, to fit them all in, two women
guests shared my parents' bedroom with my mother, while my
father came and slept in my bedroom. I had gone to bed early
and feigned sleep when he came upstairs to undress. But, from
half-closed eyes, I was both surprised and impressed to see him
kneel down by his bed in his pyjamas and spend some time in
prayer. At that time I had become very slack and indifferent
about my own prayers, but my father's example made such a
deep impression on me that I returned to the practice of daily
prayer.

Our own parish church at home, to which my mother liked
to go and to which she often took me, followed the pattern of
many Anglican churches at that time. The main service was Sung
Matins (at 11 am) and the best attended service was Evensong
(at 6.30 pm). Devout members of the congregation would attend
the 8 am service of Holy Communion once a month and at great
festivals. The services were reverent and well-ordered, but I did
not find them inspiring or inspired. The vicar was a good, hard-
working parish priest, a diligent visitor, faithful in his ministry
to the sick and dying, and reverent in his administration of the
sacraments. He was highly respected by his parishioners, even
if he did not set them alight.

It is curious how our Church seems to go from one extreme to
another. In my boyhood days the Church of England was often
accused of being cold and formal. One would hear people say,
'I have been going to this church regularly for five years and no
one has ever spoken to me.' It was an innovation for the vicar
to go to the doors of the church at the end of the service and
greet worshippers as they left.

Today some parishes put so much emphasis on fellowship
that their churches seem more like social centres than places of
worship. There is a buzz of conversation before the service
begins and no one seems to kneel down in prayer-
ful preparation.

In the Alternative Services Book (Rite A), provision is made
in the Eucharist for the 'pax'; the celebrant says: 'Let us offer

one another a sign of peace,' and all may exchange a sign of peace. I have been to some parishes where this rubric is interpreted so generously that, for five minutes, the service is interrupted while the congregation indulge in an orgy of hugging, embracing, shaking hands and kissing.

There are services where the notices giving details of social engagements last longer than any sermon or instruction. Sometimes, in such social parishes, the peaks of the liturgical year are no longer Easter, Ascension Day and Whitsun, although Christmas is celebrated with great enthusiasm, often with innumerable carol services, beginning early in December to the virtual exclusion of the season of Advent.

Instead, the parish observes a new calendar, the highlights being the autumn bazaar, the spring jumble sale, the summer outing and the harvest supper.

I have not had any experience of the charismatic services which seem the vogue with some trendy young clerics. One hears of churches which offer guitar accompaniments to hymns, clapping, waving, chanting and dancing in the aisles. These practices seem to evoke great enthusiasm, but they are so alien to the temperament of most English folk that I think they will only appeal to a minority fringe of rather odd and eccentric people.

I am thankful that in my early teens I discovered, not many miles from our home, a parish church which for years had had a Catholic tradition. It was the kind of church in which, during the week, one would often find people kneeling down in quiet prayer. There was an atmosphere of awe and reverence. The Sung Eucharist on Sundays, with full Catholic ceremonial, incense and vestments, was inspiring and uplifting. Worship there had a numinous quality; one really felt one had come into the nearer presence of God.

One of the big advantages of my boyhood home was that it was within easy reach of the headquarters of the Essex Cricket Club, then at the old Leyton ground, with its splendid wicket.

In those post-war years the county club was very hard up and could not afford many professionals. Essex frequently fielded a team consisting of eight or nine amateurs, with two or three professionals. The leading counties then were Yorkshire and Lancashire, whose teams often consisted of ten professionals with one amateur, the captain.

At that time J W H T Douglas ('Johnny won't hit today') was captain of Essex and captain of England. He had earned his nickname by a remarkable capacity for batting for a long time without scoring many runs. The Reverend F H Gillingham was a useful all-rounder and was a familiar figure at many county grounds. Percy Perrin was a mighty hitter and credited with some very big scores. G M Louden was one of the best fast bowlers in England but, as he had to work for his living, he could not play cricket very often.

Those were the days when amateurs and professionals still had separate dressing-rooms and came out of the pavilion onto the pitch by separate gates. Most summers there were several Essex players in the Gentlemen's team for the annual match against the Players at Lord's. I spent many hours watching country cricket and have happy memories of seeing, on the Leyton ground, P G Fender, Hobbs and Sandham and Strudwick of Surrey, Hendren of Middlesex and Holmes and Sutcliffe of Yorkshire. I also saw Armstrong, with his touring side of Australians.

Another great interest and enjoyment of my boyhood was cycling. In those days there was very little motor traffic in the winding Essex lanes. I am so thankful that I can remember an English countryside which still had its ancient elm trees, lanes with grass verges containing an abundance of wild flowers and hedgerows sheltering primroses and wild violets.

The countryside was very quiet then. We did not have to endure the continual roar or drone of aeroplanes flying overhead and, as few farms were mechanised, the peace of the fields was not broken by the sound of tractors. At harvest-time the sheaves stood in the cornfields and were collected by ancient haywains drawn by giant shire horses.

Largely through my cycling, I developed a love of the country-side which has been a refreshment and inspiration all my life.

Sometimes our expeditions went further afield than Essex. On one occasion, with my brother, I cycled up to Swan Pier, London, and we bought tickets for ourselves and our bicycles on the paddle-steamer which went down the Thames and on to Margate. From there, we cycled for several days, right along the south coast, visiting every village and seaside town as far as Bournemouth. Fortunately there was no Peacehaven defiling the coast road over the downs and Worthing had not yet become the capital of the 'Costa Geriatrica'.

When I was fifteen years old, I cycled on my own from London to Devonshire and was met there by my oldest brother, who had settled at Exeter. During my holiday with him, I explored a considerable part of that delectable county.

My brother had first known Devonshire during the war, when his battalion had been in billets in Exeter. As a lonely young soldier, one Sunday evening he went on his own to a local church service. Sitting near him in the pew were a kindly couple who had come with their daughter. After the service, they invited my brother back to their home for supper and before long he had fallen in love with the daughter. She was then fifteen years old and my brother was sixteen, but their teenage romance outlasted the war.

When he was demobilised, my brother was offered a job by the girl's father. His work consisted of riding round the Devonshire villages in a trap with a pony, calling on grocery shops and confectioners as a traveller representing the firm of grocery wholesalers run by his future father-in-law. He was married soon after the war and had the self-confidence, or effrontery, in his early twenties, to set up his own firm of confectionery wholesalers.

After some years he was able to sell this business and, for the rest of his working life, had a very good appointment as manager for the south-west of England of the sales force of the well-known firm of Trebor.

My other brother joined the Westminster Bank; because of a

disability in his left arm, he was not called up during the war. After my father died, in 1941, he took over the family home. He did not marry until he was forty-five, then took his bride back to share a home with my mother.

I am thankful that, for the last five years of her life, I was able to give my mother a home in my vicarage at Beaulieu. She was, I know, very disappointed that, although she had had three sons, she had no grandchildren, as both my brothers' marriages proved childless.

This means that I am the last of my family, although I am most thankful for the love and hospitality which I have been given down the years by both my sisters-in-law.

I am very fond of children and have greatly valued and enjoyed other people's children and all the opportunities I have had, in my ministry, for work with young people. But I do not think I am very possessive and do not mind not having any children of my own; it seems to me that there are too many people in the world anyhow – and I have never thought it is important that I should be reproduced.

When I was fifteen, I began to realise that I had come to a turning-point in my life. The headmaster at my school informed my father that he was wasting his money in keeping me at school. At that period fees had to be paid for secondary education unless a boy obtained a scholarship. I had lost all interest in the classes and was just wasting my time. So, at the end of the autumn term in 1921, I brought my school satchel home for the last time and began to look for a job.

The only reasons for which I can look back on my schooldays with any pleasure is that, during those years, I developed a great interest in reading and also became very fond of history. I learned to read at an unusually early age and was always rather precocious in my choice of books. Reading and history have been interests, even consuming passions, all my life and have given me many happy hours.

Looking back on the years of my time at home; although it was a very happy home, I think I was often a lonely child, despite the usual schoolboy friendships. People often look back to their childhood as the happiest time of their lives, but in my case I think it took a long time for me to sort myself out and I have been much happier as an adult. However, I look back with tremendous gratitude to my parents and my home and family.

Having now recorded my memories from my childhood onwards, I end these reminiscences with a look forward to the future and with an affirmation of my faith. I owe so much to the Church of England, which I have loved and tried to serve for so many years. But it is the Catholic faith, as taught by the Church of England, which has claimed my devotion and in which I trust.

Anglicans believe that when, in the reign of King Henry VIII, the Church of England ceased to accept the authority of the Pope, this did not involve the founding of a new church or the start of a new religion, but rather the reform of the old Church. It continued with the same creeds, the same apostolic ministry of bishops, priests and deacons, and the same major sacraments of Baptism and Holy Communion. True, its worship was reformed and simplified, and the services translated from Latin into English, steps which English Roman Catholics have also taken in recent years.

Despite the fierce antagonisms of the seventeenth century and the sloth and indifference of the Hanoverian years in the eighteenth century, the Catholic faith survived in the Church of England, as it was entrenched in the Prayer Book. In the nineteenth century it had an amazing revival and, since then, Catholic faith and practice has transformed the majority of English parishes and spread through Anglican dioceses all over the world.

Today American Protestantism is immensely rich but incredibly shallow in its teaching. Unfortunately, some liberal minded members of our Church have imported some of their vagaries into this country.

It was the Catholic faith that withstood the savage persecution of the Roman Empire and eventually overcame it. It was the

Catholic faith that faced the barbarians who overran Europe and gradually tamed and Christianised them, however incompletely. It was the Catholic faith that gradually spread all over the world, so that today there is not a continent, country or island anywhere in which the Christian religion has not been taught. It is the Catholic faith that inspired the architects and builders of Chartres, Amiens, Cologne, York Minster and so many of the world's finest buildings, as well as of innumerable beautiful parish churches. It is the Catholic faith that has inspired so many of the world's greatest painters, sculptors, musicians, poets and writers.

Today it is the Catholic faith that is mainly responsible for the overthrow of the monstrous tyranny of world Communism. The heroic resistance of Catholics in Poland, Hungary and Czechoslovakia caused the first cracks in the Soviet Empire and we are seeing the slow revival of the Eastern Orthodox Church after decades of the cruellest Russian persecution.

Until recently I had hoped that within a few decades Rome and Canterbury would again be in full communion with each other, so many of the obstacles which once divided them have ceased to exist.

But the vote in Synod in favour of the ordination of women, taken whilst I was preparing this book for publication, has brought a tragic and decisive ending to this promising movement of Christian reunion. It is interesting that the proposed legislation does not include the introduction of women bishops. The liberal establishment dare not propose this at present but undoubtedly this is the next step in the process of chipping at the foundations of the Church of England.

It is hard at the moment to see the consequences of this disastrous decision, but one thing is clear. If this catastrophic change is put into effect it will mean the end of the Church of England which I have known and loved and served. No longer will our church be the church of Augustine, Dunstan, Anselm, Sancroft, Bishop Thomas Ken, Lancelot Andrewes, Jeremy Taylor, George Herbert and Bishop King of Lincoln. It will have ceased to teach and practise the religion of the Apostolic Church and the Prayer Book, and will have adopted the ludicrous stance of pretending that the majority vote taken by the Synod of two provinces of the Church can change the nature of the ministry which the Universal Church has had for two thousand years.

Archbishop George Carey, the 103rd Archbishop of Canterbury, will go down to history as the last Archbishop of a united Church of England, and he looks like presiding over the ending of nine-hundred years of history. It is the arrogance of the liberal theologians which is so offensive. They seem to think that they know better than Our Lord Jesus Christ. He lived in a century when all the surrounding religions, pagan and eastern, had women priestesses. But He chose twelve men to be His Apostles. Our liberal bishops think they know better.

The Church of England is drifting into bankruptcy as church funds will be hard pressed to honour the promise made of compensation to all those parish priests who will have to resign on grounds of conscience; at the same time hundreds of parishes and thousands of individuals will in future withhold their contributions to central funds.

But the moral bankruptcy of the present leadership of the Church is more alarming. The issue of the ordination of women is only the last straw. For too long we have suffered from bishops who have denied vital doctrines of the Faith they have been commissioned to uphold, while retaining the emoluments and perquisites of their position. We have seen the toleration of evils like easier divorce, abortion, and the acceptance of practising homosexuals in the ministry. The time has come when we have to say, 'Enough'.

No doubt after the breach the official or compromising Church will continue. But many parish churches will become more like branches of the Women's Institute, run by women and attended by smaller and dwindling numbers of men. The cathedrals will continue, probably subsidised by State funds as tourist attractions and architectural sites, but no longer fulfilling their great task of giving spiritual teaching and being centres of devotion and worship. Bishops will no doubt continue to function on State occasions, but rather as anachronistic and colourful figures of the past like Black Rod or Gold Stick in Waiting. Parish priests will doubtless continue faithful pastoral work and the marrying and burying of a largely agnostic population. But increasingly their time will be taken up by secular and social work much like that done by Welfare State officials. It is hard to resist the conclusion that after the loss of thousands of devoted Christians the Church of England would become just a sect or a rump. It would have lost its soul.

What will become of the thousands of bishops, priests and layfolk who cannot accept the denial of the apostolic ministry by a majority vote of two provinces only of the Universal Church? Fortunately there are some months before final decisions must be taken, during which the various possibilities will be pondered, discussed and prayed about.

There may be an attempt to organise a traditionalist church within the Anglican communion consisting of those who cannot accept the ministrations of bishops who begin ordaining women. This would involve 'alternative episcopal oversight'. Priests and parishes who on grounds of conscience cannot accept women priests would no longer be under the authority of their diocesan bishop if he was in favour of this innovation. Instead there would be a network of traditionalist bishops ministering to traditionalist parishes. Another option is that advocated by Bishop Graham Leonard. If the Roman Catholic Church agreed to this, it would involve the recognition by Rome of an Anglican Uniate Church, ie a church which is part of the Roman Catholic Church but which is allowed to retain its own clergy and liturgy, and possibly some of its own customs such as married clergy. Many persons despairing of continual controversy and bickering, may just as individuals return to the 'auld Kirk'.

It seems a tragic ending to the thousand years in which the Church has ministered to the English nation and upheld the Christian faith. But at a deeper level there is no reason for sadness and despair. On the surface there seems unceasing controversy between ecclesiastics and arguments about Church structures and organisation. But underneath and unseen the Holy Spirit is continually at work. The kingdom of God is like leaven, quietly and invisibly at work until the whole world is leavened. Prayer is unceasing. Every day some individuals, warped by sin and misled by secular errors, turn back to God. Many people, having lost faith in materialism and having found no satisfaction in the excesses of the permissive age, are returning to the deep truths of the Catholic faith.

'Heaven and earth shall pass away, but My words shall not pass away,' said Our Lord, 'Lo I am with you always, even to the end of the world.'

In this faith we will go forward on our pilgrimage, praying the prayer of Christ for His followers 'that they may all be one'.